tommy walsh
OUTDOOR DIY

tommy walsh
OUTDOOR**DIY**

To my wife Marie and my kids, Charlotte, Natalie and Jonjo, for putting up with my manic lifestyle, and the fact that on the rare occasions that I am home, I'm often secreted away in my study writing.

First published in 2004 by Collins an imprint of HarperCollins*Publishers*, 77–85 Fulham Palace Road, London, W6 8JB

The Collins website address is: www.**collins**.co.uk

Text copyright © Tommy Walsh
Photography, artworks and design © HarperCollins*Publishers*
Designed and produced by Airedale Publishing

Designed and produced by Airedale Publishing Ltd
Art Director: Ruth Prentice
PA to Art Director: Amanda Jensen
Editors: Ian Kearey, Gwen Rigby
Designers: Claire Graham, Hannah Attwell
Assistants: Andres Arteaga, Anthony Mellor, Neal Kirby
DTP: Max Newton
Tommy Walsh photographs: David Murphy
Other photographs: Sarah Cuttle, David Murphy, Mike Newton, Mark Winwood
Consultant: John McGowan
Index: Emma Callery

For HarperCollins
Senior Managing Editor: Angela Newton
Editor: Alastair Laing
Design Manager: Luke Griffin
Editorial Assistant: Lisa John
Production Controller: Chris Gurney

A CIP catalogue record for this book is available from the British Library

ISBN: 0007156871
Colour reproduction: Colourscan
Printed and bound: Lego, Italy

1
outdoor basics
13

4
outdoor boundaries
85

contents

introduction

This morning it's been raining really hard, although at the moment there is a much needed respite, and this gave me food for thought about how I should introduce this book!

I was going to harp on about how we seem to be adopting a more continental attitude to our lifestyle. This is due, in part, to the change in our climate; it's becoming much warmer, with longer, hotter summers and shorter, milder winters – possibly due to global warming. (The better climate being the only positive thing to derive from global warming!)

And as our attitudes have changed, we've developed more and more leisure pursuits. One particular hobby I feel I may have had some influence on is gardening (hard landscaping) and DIY.

I feel that we are beginning to appreciate the space that we inhabit a lot more – both indoors and outdoors. So there is an inherent need to improve the space we occupy, which in turn can improve our quality of life.

I hope that you will garner some inspirational ideas as well as practical information from this book. You may have to work hard at first, but I can assure you that the benefits will be worth reaping.

tools

We all love a nice selection of power tools, and indeed they are very useful for project construction in the garden. But let's not forget the traditional tools that you need, like the fork, mattock and the humble shovel or spade.

Trowels, spirit levels, hammers and chisels, in fact all hand tools should be cleaned and wiped over with an oily rag and carefully stored until the next time they're required. Quality tools, well looked after, should last a lifetime – your lifetime – so don't loan them to anyone because they're often never returned.

LARGE TOOLS & DRILLS

always remember to read the safety information provided BEFORE use and practise before using properly for the first time

1 toolbox

2 14-volt cordless drill

3 18-volt cordless drill

4 cordless hammer drill

5 small cordless drill

6 drillbit selection

7 corded jigsaw

8 radial arm mitre saw (right)

GENERAL TOOLS

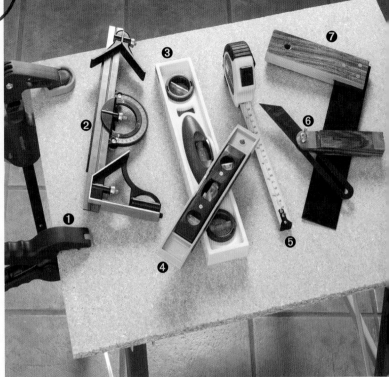

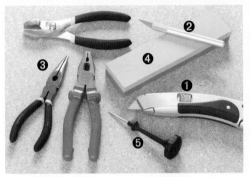

1 large craft knife	4 oilstone
2 small craft knife	5 bradawl
3 pliers & pincers	

1 clamps	4 pocket spirit level	7 set square
2 adjustable square	5 tape measure	
3 spirit level	6 sliding bevel	

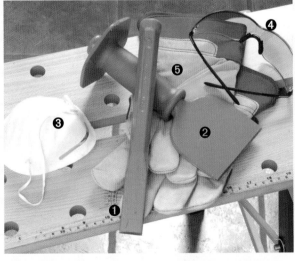

1 cold chisel	4 safety glasses
2 bolster chisel	5 gloves
3 dust mask	

safety glasses and a mask are essential for any task that could produce flying pieces

GENERAL TOOLS

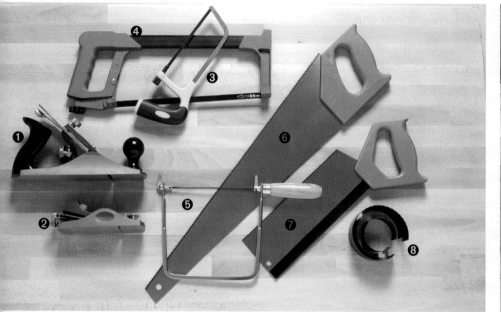

1 wood plane
2 block plane
3 hacksaw (junior)

4 large hacksaw
5 coping saw
6 hand saw

7 tenon saw
8 set of hole saws

1 claw hammer
2 chisel selection
3 screwdriver selection
4 rubber mallet
5 pin hammer

ELECTRICAL TOOLS

1 fuses
2 electric screwdrivers
3 tester screwdriver

4 long nose pliers
5 wire strippers
6 cable cutters

7 wire cutters
8 electrical testers

PLUMBING TOOLS

1 pipe cutter
2 adjustable spanners
3 plier wrench
4 gas torch
5 PTFE tape

DECORATING TOOLS

1 sealant gun	4 wire brush
2 roller & tray	5 filling knives
3 paint & masonry brushes	6 scraper

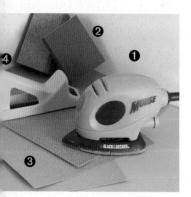

1 palm sander
2 sanding blocks
3 sandpaper
4 sander

GARDEN TOOLS

1 mattock	4 fork
2 rake	5 spade
3 shovel	6 wheel barrow

BUILDING TOOLS

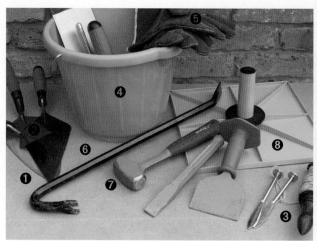

1 brick laying trowels	5 gloves
2 pointing trowel	6 crowbar
3 line & pins	7 club hammer
4 gauging bucket	8 builder's hawk

outdoor basics

Now I'm looking at you! A lot of you are saying "I'll do it some other time". Do it now! Don't make it a chore. Maintain all those gutters, brick walls, windows, doors, fences, paths and patios. Keeping your property looking and feeling great is a good financial investment and will be worthwhile in the long term. Good Luck!

maintaining your house exterior

Keeping the outside of your house in good condition not only makes it look nice, but also helps to keep out the weather. Maintenance needs to be done regularly, though, and all that painting may make you want to go out and buy PVC windows and doors!

BRICKWORK

Failed exterior walls not only look awful but can lead to other more serious problems as water penetrates through into your house. If you leave it, you only have yourself to blame. The same thing is equally relevant to your garden walls. Exterior damage can happen in two ways: either the mortar joints start to crumble and let in water, or, where masonry has lost its surface coating, water enters the porous areas and soaks into the wall. Frost will then damage the face of the brickwork; this is known to builders as 'spalling'.

If you are lucky, your wall will just need to be repointed, with the old mortar being scraped out and replaced. The advice here covers both cavity walls and older ones. Using a thin-bladed cold chisel and a club hammer, chip out any old loose mortar to a depth of about 32mm (1¼in) **1** – any loose mortar, no matter what size, must be taken out. After you have chipped out the mortar from a section of bad wall, use a stiff

brush to get out any dust and debris that is left in the joints **2**. Then go over the same area again with the brush, this time repeatedly dipping it in a bucket of water to wet the remaining mortar so the new mortar can stick to it. Mix up new mortar with 1 part cement, 6 parts builders' sand, adding water and a plasticizer to get a fairly stiff mix, and place about a shovelful on a flat board or 'hawk'. Hold the hawk against the wall, just below the joint to be pointed, and with a pointing trowel scrape some mortar off the board and press it into the joint in an upwards motion **3**, gradually working along the wall. Try to avoid getting any mortar on the bricks as it leaves horrible stains.

After about half an hour, rub gently along the freshly mortared joint with a small piece of hosepipe or copper pipe **4** to set the mortar just below the level of the brick surface. Using a soft, dry brush, gently brush away any mortar stuck to the brick surface after it has dried.

1 2 3 4

👍 **TOP TIP Always wear safety glasses when you are removing mortar, even when you are brushing away the debris – often you are more at risk from the bits flicked up by the bristles than when chipping mortar off.**

On a wall more than one brick thick, where a brick has lost its outer coating and has to be removed, use a drill and masonry bit to drill out as much mortar as possible **5**. Then use a small bolster and a club hammer to remove the rest and free the brick **6**. Replace the brick with a sound one and mortar it into position **7**. After half an hour, repoint around the brick as before and possibly around the adjacent bricks, if any mortar was dislodged there. If a number of bricks have lost their outer facing, brush the loose debris from the surface of the wall with a stiff brush dipped in water and wait for the wall surface to dry. Apply a silicone-based water repellent paint using a 150mm (6in) wide brush. Allow this first coat to almost dry before applying a second coat. Use a large brush to paint the wall, otherwise it will take you forever to do it.

👍 **TOP TIP If you are working close to a window or door, tape polythene over to protect it. It's really difficult to remove hardened silicone from these surfaces – you can simply throw the polythene away after you have finished.**

TREATING WALL SURFACES

There are times when wall surfaces can become stained or marked, leaving an unsightly discolouration. Where the markings are caused by chemicals such as grease or paint, these can be removed with the appropriate solvent-based remover, which is usually worked into the stain with a stiff-bristled brush – this is particularly important for rougher surfaces such as bricks with a wire-cut face. Wait at least 10–15 minutes for the solvent to work before washing the surface down with clear water; it's even better if you have a power-jet washer that penetrates into the cracks and crevices.

Perhaps even more of a problem is mould growth from fungi and algae, which can look terribly unsightly. This can be removed by mixing a proprietary fungicide with water and working the solution into the affected area. The mixture will need to be left for at least 24 hours to work well, and a second application may be required; allow a further 24 hours before washing the wall with clean water. It's worth checking that the masonry is sound: mouldy growths are often a symptom of an underlying damp problem, and you may be treating only the symptoms, not the cause.

Where masonry or rendering has been painted, the surface of the paint may rub off when it is touched, leaving a chalky-white deposit on your hands and clothing. This 'chalking' can be dealt with by vigorously brushing over the surface with a stiff brush **8** to remove any 'dust' and applying at least one coat of a stabilizing primer. This must be done before the wall is repainted.

5 6 7 8

MAINTAINING EXTERIOR PAINTWORK

Exterior windows and doors, eaves, woodwork, timber cladding, bargeboards and weatherboards all need some protection against the weather. Particularly if they are softwood, they need an outer coating such as paint or varnish to keep them dry and rot-proof. Remember, your painting will only be as good as your preparation, so clean off any dirt and grime, as well as old blistered or flaked paint before you start.

PREPARING TIMBER

The easiest way to remove old paint in small areas is by brushing chemical paint stripper onto the old paint **1**. Leave this for about 10 minutes, then use a paint scraper to peel away the blistered paint while it is still soft **2**. Wash down the surfaces with water after the paint has been stripped, and leave them to dry, then gently rub down the exposed wood surfaces with a palm sander **3**.

Where a surface has been painted over a number of times, and particularly if it has not been stripped down before being repainted, something more drastic than a chemical paint stripper may be called for. The most effective method is to use a blowtorch or hot-air gun to remove the layers of paint and get down to the surface of the wood below.

remember your painting will only be as good as your preparation

These tools work very well, but you must be careful. If you are using a blowtorch, you must always stroke the flame over the paint until it softens and starts to blister – do not try to burn the paint off the wood. If you are using a hot-air gun don't hold it too close to the wood and always avoid the glass. Scrape the loose paint free with a scraper. After the paint has been stripped away, sand down the surfaces to remove any paint blisters and scorch marks before applying a primer coat to the wood.

PREPARING WALL SURFACES

Rendered or pebbledashed wall surfaces and window sills are often painted with a masonry paint rather than being left a dull, grey concrete colour. Start by pressure-washing the walls or sills that are to be painted to remove any dirt or grime **4**; this will also expose any loose patches of rendering which will need to be repaired before painting starts. Where cracks are visible, run a cold chisel or filler knife along the cracks to open them slightly and give them a 'V'-shaped profile that is easier to fill **5**. Using a trowel, fill any cracks and holes with fresh mortar and allow time for this to dry **6**, **7**.

👍 **TOP TIP Mixing a small amount of PVA adhesive with the mortar will help it to bond into the filled holes and cracks and set more rapidly.**

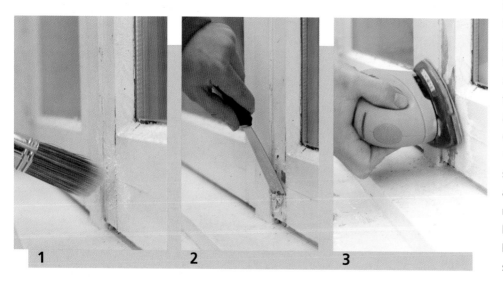

1   2   3

4

5

6

7

While it is drying, wrap newspaper around any gutters or downpipes **8**, **9** and place a layer of masking tape around the margins of doors, windows and sills to avoid them getting accidentally splattered with paint.

Where different colours are being used, invest in a roll of masking tape to protect the edges of the first paint colour applied, just before the second colour is added to the adjoining surfaces. Tape is also very handy for protecting the glass in window frames, otherwise you will spend more time wiping paint from the surfaces you don't want to paint, than painting those you do. Peel away the tape while the paint is still wet, or you may pull away the paint that has already dried. Alternatively, use a paint shield to prevent getting paint into the wrong places, and regularly wipe the edge of the paint shield with a piece of clean cloth to keep it clean.

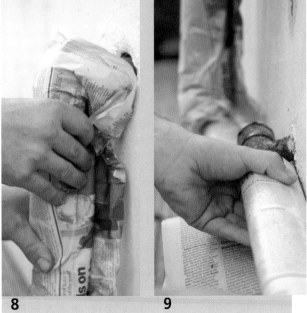

8

9

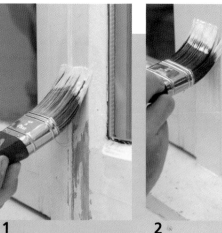

1

2

3

short vertical strokes, working the brush into the surface, and follow this with horizontal strokes to make sure you get good coverage **5**. On deeply textured surfaces, hold a stiff-bristled brush at 90 degrees to the wall and force the paint into the surface with a series of jabbing actions, **6**.

👍 **TOP TIP If you want to use a roller to apply paint to a textured wall, remember, the more coarse the wall texture, the deeper the pile should be on the roller's surface.**

PAINTING WOODWORK

Apply a primer coat to protect bare wood. Once this is dry, apply an undercoat to all surfaces **1** and allow it to dry. Apply a coat of standard (outdoor) grade gloss paint. Start with the windows, applying the paint vertically with the grain **2**, using long even strokes, before going over the horizontal areas, again with long strokes **3** to blend the paint, then blend this evenly into the areas previously painted. Finish by brushing with the grain. With weatherboards and bargeboards, always paint the undersides first and then the outsides. This stops you ending up wearing as much paint as the woodwork you are painting!

👍 **TOP TIP Start at the highest point and work down so that no dirt or rubbish can fall down onto the freshly painted surfaces below you – this saves having to do the same bit twice.**

PAINTING WALL SURFACES

Start from the top of the house and gradually work downwards using a broad brush **4**. Apply the paint using

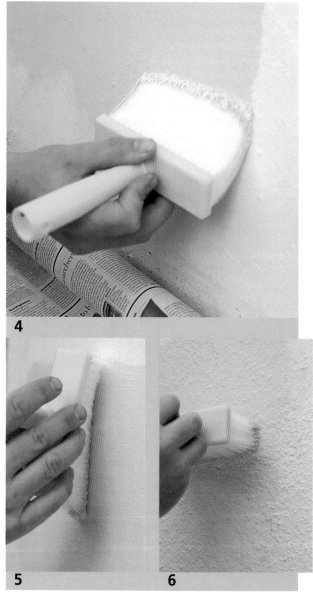

4

5

6

CLEANING GUTTERS & DRAINS

Gutters and drains should be cleaned out once a year to stop overflows or blockages. The best time is in the autumn after leaf-fall, when blockages are most likely to occur. Pick a warm day if you can, as this is always a cold, messy job, which has to be one of the most thankless maintenance jobs you can find to do, but with a bit of forethought and planning some of the most unpleasant jobs can be reduced, if not completely avoided.

Start by propping a ladder or stepladder against the wall, anchoring it safely at the base. Don't rest ladders against gutters, but hire or buy a stand-off, which fixes to the ladder and rests against the wall below the gutter. Using a garden trowel laid in the guttering, start at one end and, if possible, work towards the downpipe. Scrape out all of the dirt and debris as you go **1**, placing it in an old bucket. When all the thick debris has been removed, use a watering can full of water to wash out any remaining dirt and rubbish **2**. This will also show if there are any leaking joints. You can seal these once the guttering has dried, using a mastic gun to force a waterproof layer into the joints. Be very careful when handling pipes and gutters – the metal ones can develop sharp edges as they rust, and plastic ones become very

TOMMY'S ADVICE

A simple measure to stop leaves and debris getting into the system is a 300mm (12in) square of 12mm (½in) mesh chicken wire crumpled up into a ball and wedged into the outlets over the downpipes.

brittle after being exposed to sunlight – especially if you slip and try to hang on to one. It is also worth remembering that uPVC gutters often expand in very hot weather and many of the 'push' fittings may need some tweaking to prevent leaks when the rain comes after a spell of hot weather.

Once the gutters have been cleared and washed through, inspect the gully at the bottom of the downpipe. Remove the grid cover and, using a heavy-duty rubber glove, scoop out any debris that has built up in the gully trap **3**. If this is compacted, use an old wire coat hanger to free the rubbish. Finally, wash out the gully using a garden hose, on high pressure, before replacing the grid cover.

👍 **TOP TIP Always use a ladder or stepladder taller than you need, as it is better to have your waist level with the gutter so that you can see what you are doing.**

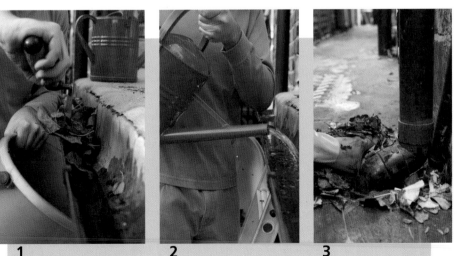

1   2   3

repairing ground surfaces

We tend to think of paths, patios, driveways and the like as permanent structures, and once they have been put in place, we just leave them – simply taking them for granted for decades, as long as they are fairly firm and we don't trip over too often.

PATIOS AND PATHS

1

2

All surfaces need some maintenance and the occasional repair, because edges crumble and slabs or blocks will crack and need replacing. At the very least, all hard surfaces need washing down at least once a year with a pressure jet or hose with a strong jet **1**. Pay particular attention to the joints because that is where the dirt accumulates and weeds can germinate and take hold.

Autumn can present real problems for a patio: the leaves won't actually harm the surface, but wet leaves make for a very slippery surface, as well as encouraging algae and moulds to grow. If the wet leaves are left piled against a wall and bridge the damp-proof course, they can cause wet patches inside the house. A leaf blower is ideal for sweeping the leaves off the patio to where they can be raked or vacuumed up, or they can be sucked up on the patio **2**.

👍 TOP TIP Using a patio cleaner once a year to scrub off the surfaces not only makes them look cleaner but removes any moss and algae, making the surface less slippery and safer to walk on.

SLABS

To replace a damaged or tilting slab, start by raking out the mortar in the joints around it with a small bolster and club hammer **3**, so you can remove the slab whole by levering it up with a crowbar **4**. If the slab is already cracked, it can be broken up with the club hammer and the pieces can be removed. Clean out the hole left by the slab, removing any mortar and concrete chips. Chisel out any remaining mortar to create a 50mm (2in) deep hole below the bottom of the slab **5**.

Mix up a small amount of mortar and spread a bed of mortar for bedding the slab **6**. Position a replacement slab on the mortar (mind your fingertips during this stage), and gently tap it down into position with a mallet, checking that it is level with the surrounding slabs. Brush a dry pointing mix into the joints around the slab **7** and wet it with a watering can before smoothing it off with a jointer and leaving it to set **8**.

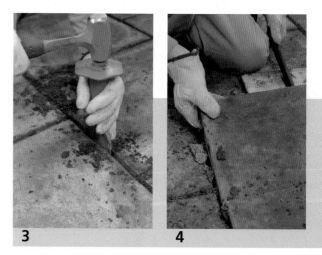

3

4

9   10   11   12

BLOCK PAVING REPAIRS

Sometimes block paving becomes uneven, as sand is washed or pushed out from beneath the blocks. This can be sorted out by lifting and re-laying a few blocks.

Place a bolster chisel between two blocks and wriggle it backwards and forwards to create a gap between the blocks **9**. Next lever out one of the blocks with a crowbar **10**; once this has been done, the others around it can be removed quite easily **11**. Remove all the blocks from the sunken area and stack them to one side. Add dry sharp sand to the area, packing it down firmly until it is at the correct level, matching that at the bottom of the surrounding paving blocks or fractionally higher **12**.

Re-lay the blocks, working from the sides into the centre of the area being repaired and packing the blocks tightly against one another as you lay them. Once an area has been repaired **13**, tip more dry sand onto the blocks **14** and brush it into the joints between them **15**. Finally, use a stout board and club hammer to tamp down the blocks until they are level with the surrounding area of paving **16**.

13   14

15   16

👍 **TOP TIP When using a crowbar as a lever, place a piece of batten on the ground to stop the bar marking the surrounding slabs – this also stops your fingers from getting trapped.**

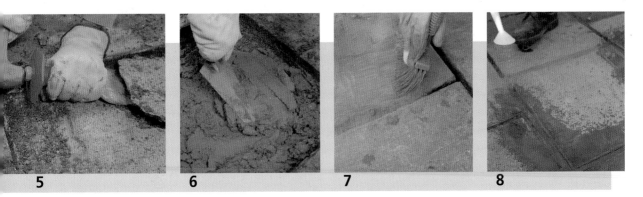

5   6   7   8

repairing posts

We all want privacy at some time. Even if we can't get the peace and quiet we would like, we can at least try to shut out the rest of the world. Often our boundaries offer physical protection from the elements, which means that they can, at times, take a real battering and given time they will need some form of repair to make good any damage.

REPLACING POSTS

Wooden fence posts are made to last, but they don't last for ever. When they do go, they usually rot at, or just below, ground level. If you need to replace a fence (or just one individual panel), it may be necessary to put one or more new posts in the same position as the old. That is usually where the fun and games start – with trying to remove the old post, especially if it was concreted in.

👍 TOP TIP **Always check each of the posts individually, as multiple posts can be loosened or cracked when a fence is damaged. It is far easier to carry out all the repairs at the same time if at all possible.**

It is advisable to bury one quarter of each new post. This will provide a firm foundation, and help the fence withstand windy conditions. Where possible, adjust the spacing of the posts in order to avoid obstructions such as the remaining concrete from previous posts.

👍 TOP TIP **When replacing a fence, start with a cut half panel, in order to avoid the concrete from the old posts.**

For posts that have to be inserted across a paved patio, lift enough slabs to dig the holes. You may need to break up sections of concrete foundations beneath the slabs to obtain sufficient depth to accommodate the

1   2   3

5   6   7   8

posts. Alternatively, it is possible to buy post 'sockets', which can be bolted into holes drilled into the patio and fitted with expanding bolts. Provided a firm anchorage can be obtained, these metal sockets will do an adequate job, although the fittings are often visible.

REMOVING AN OLD POST

Start by digging as much soil as possible from around the post to loosen it. Then drive large nails into two opposite sides of the post about 300mm (12in) above soil level **1**. Just below the nails, bind a length of stout rope around the post, leaving a loop in the end **2**. Place a large rock or a stack of bricks close to the post to use as a fulcrum to lever the post out of the ground. Place a spare fence post on the rock, with the end through the rope loop to act as a counterbalance **3**. Apply pressure to the far end of the spare horizontal post to lift it out of the ground **4**.

4

PUTTING IN A NEW POST

Dig the hole for each post, making it slightly deeper than required (usually you would want the bottom 25 per cent of the post in the ground), and place a brick or piece of paving stone horizontally in the bottom of the hole. Tap it down with the base of the post **5**. Holding the post upright, wedge bricks and rubble loosely around it **6**, and ram it firmly into place with the base of an old post or a rammer – this should be sufficient to hold the post upright. (If you are worried, attach two battens either side to keep it upright while it sets). Keep checking with a spirit level to ensure that the post is upright **7**. Add dry post-fixing concrete into the holes **8**, tamping it down with the end of a piece of batten before adding water (following the instructions on the bag). When the post-fixing concrete is sufficiently set (allow about 30 minutes), use nails or screws to fasten a pair of fence brackets to the post and put in the fence panel (see page 91). Alternatively, if you want to use your own mix (see page 36), make a stiff mix (only half the usual amount of water), and shovel this into the hole around the post. Ram it firmly into place until it is level with, or just below, the soil surface and allow it to set.

👍 **TOP TIP Where support posts are to be concreted into position, slide a 450mm (18in) section of 100mm (4in) plastic water pipe over the base of the post before it is concreted into position. Then, if the post breaks or rots, it can be removed from the pipe and replaced without digging up the concrete foundation.**

repairing gates

Ageing often has the same effect on gates as it does on people – after a certain point, they start to sag a bit. An ill-fitting gate will not open and close properly, so we tend to slam it shut, doing even more damage to the gate and gate posts.

REPAIRING METAL AND WOODEN GATES

REPAIRING METAL GATES

On the face of it, metal gates need less maintenance than wooden ones. The reality is very different, as metal gates need to be fully rust-proofed to stand the test of time. Although metal lasts a long time, it only lasts well if it's given full protection against the elements. Once that outer coating is removed or damaged in some way, the metal is vulnerable. Any slight chip or scratch that exposes the metal will enable rust to form, which will then start lifting the surrounding paint. If left untreated, this can weaken the structure of the gate.

Remove any flaking paint and rust with a wire brush **1**. For larger gates or gates that are in a very poor condition, you may need to use a powered wire brush to save time. Wear safety goggles or glasses to protect your eyes from flying flakes of paint and rust particles. Some areas of the metal may need to be rubbed down with medium grade emery paper **2** or emery cloth, to expose the bare metal.

When this thorough cleaning has been done, wipe over the metal surfaces with a cloth soaked in white spirits to get the metal surfaces completely clean **3**.

Repaint the metal with a coating of rust-inhibiting paint **4**. Usually one coat is all you need, but make sure the paint is worked well into any joints or angles where water could collect and rust is likely to form.

REPAIRING WOODEN GATES

Wooden gates will need some care and maintenance, such as a coat of wood preservative or paint each year. The hinges and latches should be oiled or greased to prevent any annoying squeaks. Where pales (the vertical boards) have become rotten, they will need replacing.

Lift the gate from its hinges and place it on a flat, level area. Remove any rotten or damaged parts and take out any rusting nails or screws. Cut and shape replacements for the discarded bits, using existing parts of the gate as templates to make sure the new additions match.

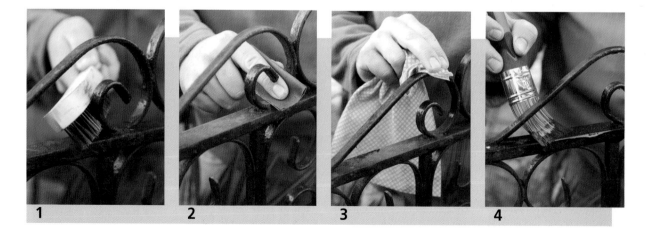

1   2   3   4

FITTING A NEW GATE

5

6

7

8

9

10

Sometimes all the repairing in the world can't get your gate back and it's time to put in a new gate and posts. Treat the new gate with at least two coats of paint or preservative to give it good protection. Start by laying the gate on the ground and placing the posts either side of it **5**, making sure they are parallel. Allow space for the catch and hinges to work. Remove the gate and nail two horizontal battens across from post to post, making sure that the lower batten is about 600–800mm (2ft–3ft) above soil level. Attach another batten diagonally between the horizontal battens **6**. These battens ensure the posts remain parallel at the correct distance apart; remove them once the posts have been concreted in. Pilot-drill and countersink the screw holes before attaching the new parts to the gate in the same place as the old ones. Dig holes for the gate posts, concrete them into position, attaching battens diagonally from each post to the ground, to keep them steady while the concrete sets.

Check to make sure they are upright **7**. The gate can now be rehung. Remember to treat the gate posts with preservative before rehanging. Fit the hinges while the gate is still laid down, then hang the gate, making sure that it swings freely **8**. Re-align the catch, marking its position and drilling pilot holes before screwing in **9**.

GATE HARDWARE OR FURNITURE

This is just a fancy name for the bits like hinges, catches, latches and closing springs that you attach to your gate. Strap hinges are generally the most popular, as they offer more support to the gate and reduce the chances of it sagging. The latch the most commonly used is the type of automatic latch that operates each time the gate is closed. This, combined with a spring closing device, which will make the gate shut automatically after someone has passed through it, is a perfect choice when young children are around **10**.

shed care & maintenance

Most of us have a garden shed – in the garden, on the allotment or sometimes both. Sheds are the perfect place to store your tools and all those other bits that you accumulate over the years, not to mention somewhere to go and disappear from the world. A place for invention and discovery, and occasional contemplation.

REPLACING SHED ROOFS AND CLADDING

Just like any other garden structure, sheds need some TLC to keep them in good condition, especially if you want them to remain weather-proof. Because sheds are exposed to the elements, the wood will split, crack and eventually rot, and roofs take a real battering from wind and rain. This often shows on the cladding, which is usually a bitumastic felt that will dry and crack. It turns very brittle in the sun and will eventually tear in the wind and let in water, unless it is replaced.

RE-FELTING A SHED ROOF

Keep the roll of felt in a warm place for about a week before you use it. Warming the new felt improves its flexibility and it becomes much more pliable. Pick a dry day **1**. You will need a step-ladder to gain access to the roof, and it is best to remove boards with a claw hammer **2**, **3**. Rip off the old felt. If it is already torn, just pull off as much as you can reach. Ease out

any old nails still holding it on **4** plus any fragments of felt. Then pull off the felt until the roof is completely clean **5**. If any mastic has been used, you may need to use a paint scraper to lift the felt. Check the roof cladding boards and replace any that look worn.

Roll out the new felt on the ground (with the outer surface face down to the ground) and cut it to length using a craft knife with a batten as a straight edge. Leave a surplus of 80–100mm (3½in–4in) at each end of the felt for fastening it down. Roll up the measured section of felt and take it up onto the roof. Position the felt on the roof **6** and nail it down along the edge (eaves) of the roof with round-headed felt nails (clout nails) **7**, before folding the felt along the front and back end of the roof **8** and nailing it firmly into position **9**. Repeat this process on the other side of the roof. Cut a narrow strip to cover the

1

2

3

4

5

6

7

8

9

10

11

ridge of the roof and allow an overlap of at least 80–100mm (3½in–4in) over the felt that is already nailed down **10**. Spread a layer of felt mastic onto the felt to act as an adhesive **11** and roll out the narrow strip of felt to form a 'ridge cap', pressing it firmly into place over the mastic. Felt nails can be positioned about 25mm (1in) back from the edge of the felt to provide extra anchorage **12**. Finally, nail down any overhung edges **13** and trim away any surplus felt with a retractable craft knife **14**.

👍 **TOP TIP Rolls of felt are heavy, so rather than try to lift an entire roll onto the roof, measure the sections, cut them to length and carry these up to the roof.**

For larger roofs where more than one strip of felt will be needed on each roof panel, always start at the bottom of the roof, working up towards the ridge. This way, the second strip of felt will overlap the first one, which is the correct method for shedding water. Also, for large roofs, wooden strips are often nailed onto the felt to secure it onto the roof and stop it lifting – these strips run down the roof.

12

13

14

1

2

3

👍 TOP TIP When replacing cladding boards, always ease them up gently. If the wood interlocks, you can easily damage the boards that neighbour the one you wish to replace. Be patient here, or you could finish up having to replace half your shed wall.

4

5

REPLACING CLADDING BOARDS

The roof and walls of a shed are usually made from panels of tongue-and-groove (or overlapping) strips of wooden cladding nailed onto a wooden stud frame. Occasionally, some of these boards get damaged or rot and will need to be replaced.

To remove any rotten or damaged parts, gently force a screwdriver or crowbar between the cladding board and support frame, levering the board free **1**, then lift it off **2** and remove any rusty nails or screws. Saw a new board to length and slot it into position, before nailing it firmly into place **3**. Paint over it with a wood preservative, including the bottom edge and any side edges that are visible.

ROUTINE CARE

Many minor repairs can be avoided if the shed's side and end walls are cleaned and painted every year.

Start by brushing down the dry wood with a stiff brush to remove any dirt and algae, and also lift off any flaking paint with a scraper or wire brush **4**. Fill small holes or cracks with a silicone sealant **5**. Working from the top of the wall downwards, use a brush to apply wood preservative or paint, working it into the surface with vertical and horizontal strokes **6**, following the direction of the cladding boards to get good coverage. Work plenty of preservative into the joints between the boards where any water is likely to collect. If the paint dries leaving a blotched appearance, apply a second coat, and pay particular attention to any exposed areas where the wood is cut across the grain.

6

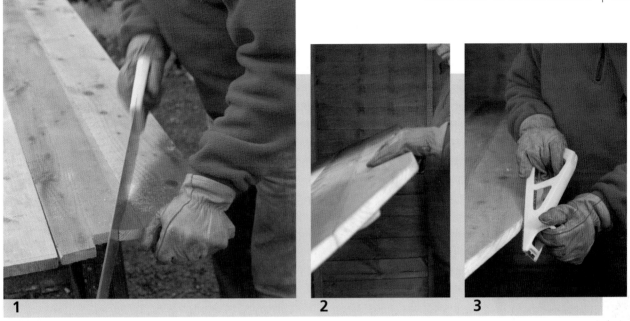

1   **2**   **3**

FITTING OUT A SHED

A garden shed is usually much more than just a garden shed. It has a variety of functions, mainly for working or storage, such as:

- potting shed
- work and repair shop
- tool store
- machinery store
- chemical store
- garden sundries store

The uses often change depending on the time of year, with the shed becoming a store for garden furniture, barbecues and the like through the winter months. For most of us, it does not matter what size shed we think we need – we usually manage to accumulate so much stuff that, almost immediately, the original shed is too small. With this in mind, it is important to try and organize the space to get as much as possible stored inside, but still have room to work.

WHAT DO YOU NEED?

Well, this all depends on what you want to use the shed for, but if you are going to work in it, you will almost certainly need a workbench. If you do put in a bench, its position needs a bit of thought, as ideally the top of the bench should be just above waist height to stop you having to stoop too much when you are working. If you have a window in the shed, put the bench on the same side so that you get the best possible natural light in the area where you are working.

When it comes to storage, arrange tools so that they are neat and tidy and positioned to make the best use of the space available. The obvious solution, which gardeners have used over the years, is to hang the tools on the wall – well, with all that space, you have to use it, and cover the cladding, don't you?

FITTING A BENCH

Measure the inside of the shed and cut three 150mm (6in) wide gravel boards to length, and then fasten them together with screws and battens on the underside. If the bench is going to obstruct the doorway, taper the end with an angled saw cut **1**. Screw two horizontal battens to the inside of the shed walls to support the bench top when it is slotted into position inside the shed **2**, and use a plane or rasp to trim away any rough edges on the bench top and front **3**.

STORAGE

In most garden sheds, the floor space is precious and the walls are largely under-used. Many garden tools are fairly flat, and have straight stems and handles, so they can easily be hung onto the bare walls.

👍 **TOP TIP If the walls of your shed are made from thin timber, fasten battens or flat boards onto the inside walls before fixing tool hooks or supports onto them 1.**

Fasten the tool hooks onto the wall with woodscrews, positioning them at such a height to be sure that the tools are hanging up rather than resting on the floor, and allowing enough room to be sure that each tool hangs free of its neighbours.

Smaller hooks or brackets can be used to keep smaller tools, such as hammers, pliers and screwdrivers tidy – these are often hung on the walls above the workbench, to make better use of the space and keep them handy for when you need them **2**.

👍 **TOP TIP To put your tools away quickly at the end of a job and to make sure you can find exactly the correct tool for the next task, draw around the tool and there will be no mistake where to put it!**

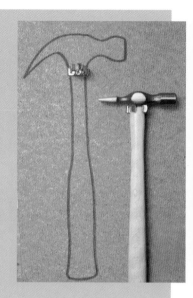

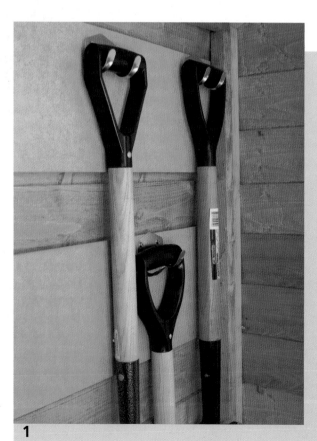

1

2

TOMMY'S ADVICE

Once you have put a bench inside your shed, the space underneath it is perfect for storing pots and compost (below), even a small mower if you have one. However, do allow enough room for your feet to fit under the bench when you are working. Come the winter, you can store all the garden chairs and neatly tuck away the barbecue and still be able to work at the bench (right).

calculating your materials

One of the biggest headaches for the DIYer is calculating how much foundation material you need: how much mortar, how many slabs, bricks, setts etc. If you don't have a head for maths, my tables will hopefully give you some help, but always have a calculator to hand.

CHOOSING YOUR MATERIALS

A good path or patio is judged, not on how good it looks, but more on how long it lasts before developing cracks or defects such as crumbling or sagging. Usually, how well these last depends on how well they were constructed. The base and sub-base foundations will be the most important factors in determining how long and how well your surface lasts and stays in good condition.

HOW TO ESTIMATE

For most people who take on construction projects in the garden, the real worry is not the work, it is the planning and organisation before the physical work starts. For many, by far and away the most daunting task is estimating – the calculation of what materials are needed to complete a particular job, mainly because it is a task which is undertaken very occasionally, providing little opportunity to become practised and confident. You need to know exactly how much you need to buy before you go to the superstore.

On the one hand, there is the nagging fear of running out of materials partway through the job and the necessity of stopping work to go and get more. Balanced against this is the dread of having a leftover pile of sand or stack of bricks blocking the driveway, or a bag of cement going hard in the garage. Having a working plan of your intended project drawn on graph paper can make calculations easier – you can count up the squares and then use the charts to find out exactly what you need.

As far as calculating for decking is concerned, it is easy to calculate the framework, but only an accurate plan of your deck will help you calculate the number of timber, screws etc (see opposite).

FOUNDATIONS FOR STEPS

With steps, the key issue is to construct the steps as a whole unit – a flight of steps (which is better able to withstand the downward pressure) rather than lots of individual steps (which the pressure can cause to sink/lift). In the main, the same rules apply as for paths: the looser the soil, the deeper the foundations need to be. However, if the recommendation is for a foundation depth of 150-200mm (6–8in), it is usual to err on the side of caution and go to a depth of 200mm (8in).

CALCULATING FOUNDATIONS

The big difficulty with estimating the foundation depths, especially for large, flat areas like patios and paths, is that it depends largely on the soil type. Heavier, compacted soils do not need such a great depth of foundation – often 50% less than a light, loose soil. A mixture of 6:1 (six bags of ballast to one bag of cement) is required for decent foundations. The chart opposite relates to the number of 50kg (110lb) bags of ballast and cement to buy. DIY stores sell their cement and ballast in standard bag size now, and have rounded up the figures so that the metric and imperial marry. Once you know the square metrage of your area and the depth of foundation you need, use the chart to calculate how many bags.

Now this is not an exact science, but here is an example. The patio is 5sq.m (5⅛sq.yd), for which you need 150mm (6in) foundations. The chart gives you a figure of 40 bags. Divide 40 by seven, which is very roughly five. Multiply that number by one for cement and seven for ballast. Your final tally will be five bags of cement and 35 bags of aggregate = 40 bags!

PATIOS AND PATHS – HARD MATERIALS COVERAGE (IMPERIAL IN BRACKETS)

	To cover 1sq.m (1⅛ sq.yd)		
Materials – number required	**Bricks** (laid flat)	36	(43)
	Bricks (laid on edge)	54	(64)
	Block paviors	39	(46½)
	Slabs 610 x 610mm (2 x 2ft)	2.75	(3⅓)
	Area	**sq.m**	**(sq.yd)**
Materials – area covered	**1000 bricks** laid flat	25*	(30)
	1000 bricks laid in rows on edge	16.5*	(20)

*if patterned surfaces are required, due to cutting, reduce the area covered by 1.5sq.m (1⅘sq.yd)

PATIOS AND PATHS – LOOSE MATERIALS COVERAGE (IMPERIAL IN BRACKETS)

	Area	sq.m	(sq.yd)
Materials – 1 tonne (1 ton) will cover	**Setts** 100 x 100mm (4 x 4in)	4	(4¾)
	Cobbles 50 x 75mm (2 x 3in)	7	(8½)
	Gravel 25mm (1in) deep (loose)	30	(36)
	Gravel 50mm (2in) deep (rolled)	12	(14½)

CALCULATING DECKING FRAMEWORK

To calculate the timber needed, measure the width and length of area to be covered. Work out the number of joists you will need for the whole framework. For joists over 3m (10ft) allow for a transverse brace every 2m (6ft) to stop warping. For the decking boards, work out the number of boards you will need from the dimensions of the boards you are using. Remember to allow for a gap of about 6mm (¼in) between the boards.

TOMMY'S ADVICE: SAFETY RULES

In order to avoid any nasty surprises when digging out soil for fence posts or foundations or etc, you should know the minimum depths of the main domestic services which you are likely to encounter.

MINIMUM DEPTHS OF SERVICES (imperial in brackets)

Water mains	910mm (3ft)
Gas	610mm (2ft)
TV/telephone cables	510mm (1ft 8in)
Electricity cables	760mm (2ft 6in)
Main sewers under grass	910m (3ft)
Main sewers under hard surfaces	1.2m (4ft)

VOLUME CALCULATOR FOR FOUNDATIONS (IMPERIAL IN BRACKETS)

For garden paths and patios you need 75–150mm (3–6in), for driveways and car turning points 150–300mm (6–12in).

	Area	1sq.m (1⅛sq.yd)	5sq.m (5⅛sq.yd)	10sq.m (10¼sq.yd)	50sq.m (59sq.yd)
Depth of foundation	**75mm (3in)**	0.08cu.m (4 bags) (1⁄16cu.yd)	0.4cu.m (20 bags) (½cu.yd	0.75cu.m (40 bags) (¾cu.yd)	3.75cu.m (200 bags) (4½cu.yd)
	150mm (6in)	0.15cu.m (8 bags) (⅛cu.yd)	0.75cu.m (40bags) (¾cu.yd)	1.5cu.m (80 bags) (1⅗cu.yd)	7.5cu.m (400 bags) (8cu.yd)
	300mm (12in)	0.3cu.m (16 bags) (⅖cu.yd)	1.5cu.m.(80 bags) (1⅗cu.yd)	3 cu. m.(160 bags) (3⅘ cu.yd)	15cu.m (800 bags) (16cu.yd)

patio & path foundations

Paths and patios should last a long time, but how much wear and tear they can absorb depends as much on the quality of the foundations as on the quality of the surface – even the most expensive paving slabs will make a disappointing surface if the base is substandard.

CHOOSING YOUR FOUNDATIONS

Foundations provide the main substance and strength to your patio, while the surface layer provides some of the support, but all of the decorative finish.

The type of foundation you will need depends on the amount of traffic it is likely to carry, and what sort. For the average garden patio, which will only have people walking and sitting on it (and perhaps the occasional wheelbarrow-load), the foundations do not need to be particularly substantial. A simple base of a sand/cement mixture laid onto compacted soil may be quite adequate, although a sub-base of concrete will substantially strengthen the base.

👍 **TOP TIP The more time you spend on the foundation stage, the fewer problems you are likely to encounter when you begin to lay the patio, and this is particularly important when you are setting levels.**

Where the patio is adjacent to a building, it is important that the slope or 'fall' runs away from the building. This angle does not need to be steep; 1 in 100 = 1cm in 1m (about ½in per 3ft) is quite adequate. Also, the top surface of the patio should be at least 150mm (6in) below the level of the building's damp-proof course, to prevent moisture bridging this layer and causing damage to your property.

LEVELLING THE GROUND

Start by marking out the shape of the paved area using a string line and wooden pegs **1**, or use a special spray for marking out **2**. When marking out with pegs, use a spirit level to make sure that you get the desired amount of fall across and along the edges of the path or patio – it is essential to get the levels set before construction starts **3**. Strip off any turf or plant material from within the marked area **4**. Dig out the soil to a depth of about 150mm (6in), which is the correct depth for areas that are to be used for heavy pedestrian traffic **5**.

1

2

3

6   7   8

Rake and tamp down the excavated area until it is roughly level, and compact the soil at the base with a stout wooden post, rammer or heavy rake. If you are paving a large area, consider hiring a plate vibrator which can be used to compact the area. Cover the excavated area with a layer of scalpings **6** or well-broken rubble and compact this down to a depth of about 50mm (2in) **7**, followed by a 50mm (2in) layer of compacted sand **8**.

Use a board or plank with a straight edge to check that the sand or concrete is level over the whole area. Drawing a section of board across the patio base is a very good way of spreading the sand evenly **9** – the board will scrape off any humps and draw the surplus sand into any hollows that may be left. Keep checking that the levels are correct **10**. Getting the foundation right makes life much easier when you start laying the surface.

9

it is important that the slope runs away from any buildings

4   5   10

tommy's magic mortar mixes

To make a path or patio, lay the slabs on a bed of mortar about 50mm (2in) thick. Mix the mortar with enough water to make it soft and pliable but not wet and runny. A little standard plasticizer added to the mix will keep it pliable for longer.

MORTAR MIXTURE

MORTAR BED MIX
4 parts sharp sand
2 parts soft sand
1 part cement
water
plasticizer

POINTING MIX
3 parts dry soft sand
1 part cement

1

2

3

4

5

To make a mortar bed, combine the two sands **1**, then mix together thoroughly with the cement **2**. Make a well in the centre and add water **3**. Mix it together until it is soft and pliable **4**. Add some plasticizer to the mixture to create the perfect bedding mix. The mortar is now ready for action **5**.

outdoor planning

Planning is important, so take your time, and don't just plan for the present, plan for the future! Include the whole family in the consultation process, and give responsibility for an area of the garden to each family member.

planning a new garden

Whether you are planning to make a new garden or revamp your old one, one thing you need to consider is whether or not to employ a garden designer. In the end, it's you who has to live with the garden after the work has been done. If you have the time, it's much more fun to plan and develop your own garden – but don't rush, this isn't like moving the furniture in the lounge, it's much more permanent.

OVERALL CONSIDERATIONS

A particular style of garden, for example a low-maintenance garden, might be a priority for those with less time to spend gardening than they would like. Even the functional aspects, such as where the washing is dried or the rubbish is stored, should be taken into account and worked out before deciding on what type or style of garden you would like.

WHAT DO YOU WANT?
Start by making a list of what you would like in your garden. This list will always be much larger than your garden can cope with, but you can gradually whittle it down to the essentials, such as:
✔ a shed for storing tools
✔ a greenhouse
✔ a patio or deck for sitting and eating outdoors
✔ a path leading to the main parts of the garden
✔ fences or hedges for privacy
✔ a play area or sand pit for younger children
✔ a fruit or vegetable plot

Start by collecting articles and pictures that match your ideal look: get ideas from the numerous gardening magazines and watch the television programmes that show you how to do it. Those that show you how to transform your garden in three days will give you plenty of food for thought – but don't expect miracles!

TAKING STOCK
When you've run out of excuses and it's finally time to tackle the garden, don't fall into the tempting trap of ripping everything out, clearing the site and starting from scratch. This approach can be really wasteful in terms of plants, resources, time and money – and unless radical changes are absolutely necessary, it is best avoided.

The wisest approach is to wait a year to see what happens in the garden – this is also called postponing the inevitable. This will give you time to pick out the plants you would like to keep and label them so that you don't rip them out by accident. Divide the plants and features into 'need to keep', 'nice to keep' and 'got to go'.

Garden features in the 'nice to keep' list often include materials that can be used in another way or recycled: you can save time and work if your old patio has broken slabs, because it could become the foundation for a new wooden deck; old bricks and paving left over from structures that have been ripped out can be used as a sub-base for new paths or foundations; and discarded timber can be used as shuttering for concrete, with smaller bits re-used as marker pegs.

WHERE TO START?
Once you've written down your wish list for the garden, it's time to start working out how it'll all fit. You need to draw up a basic plan – nothing fancy, but it must be reasonably accurate or things will go wrong once you start work. Use a large plain-paper notebook or graph paper and always work in pencil (we all make mistakes!).

Use a long tape measure to take measurements **1**, or get one person to stride them out (no two people have the same step length, so use the same person every time).

1

1

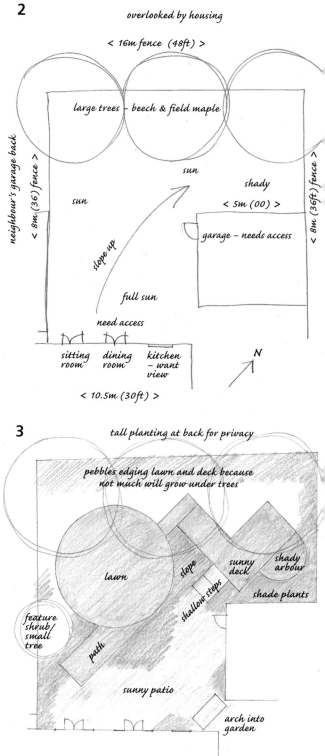

Start by measuring from a fixed point, like the side of the house, and 'tie in' each point by measuring to it from at least two places, to ensure accuracy. Make sure you take the measurements of any fixtures that are going to stay.

Make sketches in the garden as you go **1**, drawing in the boundaries of the garden and the position of the house. Then add any features that will stay, like a shed or greenhouse; this will give you a much clearer idea of the area you are working with. Mark on the plan which direction the garden faces so that when you come to plant, you won't put a tree where it will shade the patio, or put shade-loving plants in full sun **2**.

You can also cut out shapes to scale, to represent all the features you want to end up with in the garden and move them around on the plan to get the best combination. When you're happy, you can draw around them onto the plan and add linking features like paths. Finally, draw up the garden to scale on a large sheet of paper, again with that pencil. You could add a little colour now to give you an idea of hard and soft features like decking and lawns **3**. If you find that you are not able to get the result you want, you may want to bring in a professional to draw a plan **4**. You can ask around, look in the back of local magazines or ask at a horticultural college or your local garden centre for a list of designers. But doing this doesn't come cheap. You can keep the costs down by just using their plans and then doing all the work yourself.

KEEPING THINGS IN SCALE

The main problem with most gardens, especially ones belonging to new houses, is their size. They are never as big as a gardener would like, so the trick is to make the best use of what you've got so the end result isn't top-heavy.

Try to balance each area of planting with an equal area of open space so you have room to see it. Link different parts of the garden with open areas or paths, so that as you walk around it, the design seems to connect and 'flow'.

Ideally, you should try to hide parts of the garden so that it can't all be seen at once, but in a small area, that's not easy to do. What you can do is vary the planting height as you go down the garden, rather than always having low plants at the front of the border and taller ones at the back.

DECEIVING THE EYE

You can't do much to change the shape or size of the garden, but you can change how you see it. A long, thin garden can be made to seem wider by laying paving from side to side rather than running lengthways. Brightly coloured flowers at the far end will make that end seem closer, especially if they are large ones, whereas small, paler ones near the house will make the garden feel more spacious.

This principle also works in reverse. Small, pale-coloured flowers at the end of a short garden will make it recede into the distance, particularly if larger, brighter ones are used near the house.

4

N

try to balance each area of planting with an equal area of open space so you have room to see it

CHOOSING YOUR FEATURES

As you decide on your design, bear in mind that some features are more practical than others and will need to be placed carefully. The washing line really needs to be accessible from a path, or you will end up with wet feet.

LOOK AFTER THE SOIL

Gardeners love their soil, it provides the raw material in which they can grow their plants but, as a builder, I think it makes a very good surface to dig foundations into and lay paths and concrete on.

The major limitation on what you can grow in your garden is the soil. Soil is the raw material of any garden, but certain plants prefer to grow in certain soils, and although many can cope with less-than-ideal conditions, they just don't grow as well as they should. If your soil is in good condition, then the plants will be able to look after themselves, making less work for you!

soil pH

One of the main factors limiting the type of plants a garden will support is the soil pH. This affects the availability to plants of the minerals present in the soil. The scale goes from 0 – 14 (7 is neutral) and is used to measure how acidic or alkaline (limy) the soil is. Knowing the result will help you to select the best plants for your garden. Testing the soil pH can be done very easily with a simple ready-to-use kit that you can buy from most garden centres.

soil drainage

How well the soil drains can also affect the plants that will grow well in your garden. To find out if the soil is poorly drained, start by digging a hole 600mm (2ft) deep and look at the colour of the soil on the spade **1**, especially from the lower levels.

Soil that is smelly and bluish-grey in colour has been suffering from a lack of air – a sure sign of poor drainage. This will restrict your plants' root growth, and they will form only a shallow root-system and will suffer from drought in dry summer periods, as the upper level of soil dries out quickly.

soil improvement

The better the condition of the soil, the better the plants in it will grow. Digging manure or compost into the garden will always improve your soil. This is ideal for long-term improvement, because as they decompose,

1

they contribute to the formation of humus within the soil, which then retains the other applied nutrients like fertilizers.

CLEARING AND SORTING

At some stage, you will need to start doing some clearance. As you work, you will most likely make a mess – it's inevitable – but the more you can minimize this, the easier it will be to do the job.

As you start to clear an area, try to work systematically and mark off certain areas as collection points for various types of material being cleared – this makes sorting for recycling or dumping much easier, as well as keeping things organized and reasonably tidy. Have a skip on standby for the stuff you really don't want to keep.

Finally, as you work, keep that picture in your mind of the perfect lawn, the beautiful patio **2** and you sitting there admiring your work in the late afternoon sun, with a long cooling gin and tonic in hand!

garden features

It is worth viewing hard surfaces as a whole, as you can't really separate paths and walkways from patios and steps, because they are usually linked together and form a framework for the garden. You need to choose what surface to use. Then you need to think about the boundaries, and, finally, those finishing touches – lighting, furniture and maybe even a water feature.

PATIOS

PATTERNS AND DESIGNS

Patterns should be clear and simple – the key to good design is to avoid mixing too many different materials, as this gives a busy, distracting effect. However, large areas of one single material in one unit size can be static and monotonous, but they are ideal for a small patio **1**. On a practical level, there are some materials that should be avoided in certain situations – granite setts and cobbles are not good surfaces for a patio or seating area because their uneven surface makes it difficult to keep furniture stable. Gravel can be dry, dusty and unstable – not ideal in a seating area. The smaller grades of gravel and slate can be picked up on footwear and carried indoors, and they can encourage cats to turn your garden into a communal litter tray, but gravel is popular for security, since it is impossible to walk over it quietly.

1

2

👍 TOP TIP: PATIO PATTERNS

Lay even-sized stone paving with red brick or granite setts to contrast the colour and texture of the stone and to break up a simple squared pattern **2**, **3**, or use setts in curves to create a pleasing pattern **4**. Different sized York stone paving creates a simple patio. You can vary the spaces between the paving to create planting pockets. Alternatively forget squares and convention and incorporate planting and even grass in your design **5**, with the stones below the grass for problem-free mowing.

4

3

5

PATHS

Paths are usually taken for granted in the garden and are seen simply as a means of moving around without getting your feet wet – functional, but not very ornamental.

In fact, a path can link parts of the garden together, as well as linking house and garden, and you can choose the materials that create movement and flow within the garden. In small gardens, creating a winding path makes the journey through the garden seem longer **1**, while gravel or cobbles are good at drawing the eye along a curved path **2**.

2

1

Bricks and blocks laid lengthways along a path invite forward movement, and create the illusion that the garden is longer than it is **3**. Shaped wood with gravel insets makes a striking surface **4**, and decking squares can also be used for small areas **5**, perhaps joining up with a deck. Large slabs of York stone or concrete paving laid along the surface can create an irregular, interesting effect **6**. Edging with a different material breaks up regular plain paving **7**. Laid across the garden or patio, cobbles, bricks **8**, slates **9**, and setts are ideal for creating a feeling of width, as the small units are perfect for making patterns.

Whatever materials you use, the ground will need thorough preparation before you begin laying a path or patio (see page 34).

3

4

5

6

7

8

9

SLOPES AND RAISED AREAS

A truly level garden is very rare, which is not necessarily a bad thing, apart from the fact that we always seem to want the garden that we don't have. Obviously, there are degrees of sloping garden, ranging from the gentle slope through to the steep 'suitable for a mountain goat' garden, where terraces need to be built to garden at all.

Tackling a sloping garden can seem a frightening prospect, but the best approach is to view the slope as an opportunity rather than a problem, especially if you try working with the slope rather than trying to fight it. This is a battle you are never going to win – so compromise and use the slope to create a garden you can cope with and enjoy **1**.

Paths can be more interesting in a sloping garden **2**, simply because you have to consider the slope as part of your route in rather than just how to get from A to B the most direct way. The height and distance between any steps will vary according to the angle of the slope – steps will be much closer together on a steep slope **3** and farther apart on a gentle one. You can even have a stepped or terraced lawn if you want – all of which makes for interesting features, not problems.

The most important thing to remember about working on a slope is that any steps, walls or other structures you build must be very well made, to cope with pressures that structures on level sites do not have.

2

1

3

4

5

6

the most important thing about working on a slope is that anything you build must be very well made

On a slope, the soil is constantly moving – not by any great amount, but it does not keep still – and there is always gradual but constant pressure pushing down from the top of the slope. So when you build walls or steps, try to provide as much anchorage as possible, so your construction can withstand these pressures for as long as possible.

Where a structure has a flat surface, such as a step, you should always build in a very slight slope or tilt to the downhill side, to shed water. If you allow water to build up behind the structure, this will help increase pressure and eventually result in slippage.

If you have a level plot or just a gentle slope, you can still vary the height levels within your garden by creating raised beds **4**, **5**, **6**, which provide ease of access or seating, as well as allowing different types of raised border. These beds are ideal if you are unable to bend very far or are confined to a wheelchair, and they are really useful when you have very heavy, sticky clay soil, because you can just build your border or bed on top of it using good topsoil brought in from elsewhere.

BOUNDARIES

As the size of the average garden continues to shrink and most of us live close together in a town or city environment, we tend to value our privacy more than ever before. When the garden is used as a place in which to relax, there is a natural tendency to try to have at least one section that is not overlooked, to create a sense of seclusion, and this can usually be achieved by some form of screening.

The boundary of the garden is where we usually stake our claim to 'our' property. A fence is an excellent low-cost alternative to a wall and provides cover much more quickly than even the most vigorous hedging plants possibly could. There are some situations where a fence may be appropriate, and there are many materials and patterns that can be used, such as bamboo and natural wood **1**, **2**, and **3**.

The purpose of the fence may influence the type to be erected and the material to be used. For instance, where the fence is to provide a visual, rather than a physical barrier, an open fence is an excellent choice **4**, as it is ideal for training plants along. Ranch, interwoven wood **5** and hazel hurdles, are all good for wind protection, and larch-lap is ideal for privacy.

Where shelter is the main aim, there are two things you need to consider. First, you can't stop the wind, you have to filter or divert it in some way to reduce its speed – a 'porous' screen, which allows some wind through at a reduced speed will work, but a solid barrier will not **6**. And secondly, in an open, exposed garden you will need to use extra long posts that will stay upright if the wind gets really strong, and maybe even some angled wooden braces on the inside of the fence to push against the wind and provide more strength.

👍 **TOP TIP Remember that most local authorities will restrict the height of a solid fence or screen such as larch lap or interwoven panels – you can usually erect to about 2m (6½ft) high. If you have nosy neighbours, put a section of open structured trellis on top of the fence, then just plant climbers to fill in the gaps in the trellis.**

1

2

3

5

4

6

SCREENS & TRELLIS

The one modern trend is to see the garden as an outdoor room or, if your garden is larger, a series of rooms. This is great until it rains but no one ever mentions roofs, just walls for these 'outdoor rooms'! Seriously, screens and trellis make great dividers to split up the garden and hide or disguise things you would rather not see; or they will make you travel further into the garden to see what else there is, simply because the screen is blocking your view.

The intended purpose of a screen will influence the type and materials to be used and how it is erected. A visual, rather than a physical barrier is often required, and light screens or trellis **1** could be used so that a view is only partly obscured, offering some idea of what is beyond, and playing to our natural instincts to be nosy

and want to see more. Where something is to be hidden **2**, you need a screen with a 'close weave' that almost totally obscures the object you are embarrassed by – that dustbin or compost heap, which are the elements of the garden we most commonly want to hide. After all, they are hardly tourist attractions. Wattle hurdles or low sections of lap screening are perfect in these situations.

1

2

If you can, avoid using solid barriers. These will need extra-strong posts and are likely to get damaged, especially on windy sites where they block, rather than filter the wind, so they can take a real battering. Also, these barriers will cause the wind to swirl, which can cause havoc with your plants around the garden, often doing more damage than just a strong wind coming from one direction.

One of the main reasons for the popularity of trellis is because it provides a screening structure while allowing plants to grow up and through it **3**, **4**, which tends to form the best camouflage for hiding or disguising views or objects. It also offers a vertical surface for plants to grow up – a simple way of adding height in a garden.

👍 **TOP TIP Structures like trellis, which are very open, allow much more light to filter through and create far fewer shadows than more solid screens or fences. This encourages plants to grow towards or through them, rather than away from them, which is what happens with closed weave or solid screens.**

3

4

ARCHES AND PERGOLAS

If you have a small garden or you are a bit stuck for space and want to grow more than you have room for (let's face it, nearly all of us do), you can always resort to 'vertical gardening'. This is particularly useful on a flat site where there would otherwise be little above ground level, especially if you don't have room to grow trees. There is a limit to what you can grow up a wall or fence, assuming you have access to them, so look at other upright structures, such as arches, obelisks and pergolas, to provide a growing surface.

Where height is going to be used, particularly if the garden space is small, try to choose a structure that adds space, rather than occupying it. This makes the design and choice of materials very important. If the structure is too heavy, it will look big and clumsy, and cast heavy shade, and it may spoil some of the plants growing close by. In an ideal world, most shadows should be cast by the foliage of plants growing up the structure. The thickness of the legs and cross-rails will affect what can be grown up the structure, since the larger these pieces are, the less likely it becomes that climbing plants will be able to attach themselves to them. On the other hand, any structure you build must be strong enough to cope with the weight of plants in full leaf – even during wet or windy conditions. Bear in mind that the structure needs to be the correct size so as to keep it in scale with its surroundings in the garden, rather than totally dominating them.

1

ARCHES
These structures usually straddle a path or walkway **1**, **2** and can be as simple or complicated as you like, but they must be big enough for you to walk under without having to duck or stoop and wide enough not to get your clothing caught on the plants at the sides. The basic structure consists of four upright sections that form the main support, with horizontal or angled cross beams to form the overhead structure or roof, linking one side of the arch to the other. The sides can be filled in with

vertical or horizontal timbers that are thinner than the main uprights, or you can use trellis to fill in the side panels and the roof if you wish **3**.

PERGOLAS
These are often a collection of arches arranged along a path or walkway and linked together along the line of the path either with timber or sometimes with thick rope loops or 'swags' for plants to grow along **4**. Also, with more gardens having decks or patios, pergolas can be one-sided, attached to a house on one side with posts supporting the overhead beams on the open side. The roof between the main overhead beams can be filled in with trellis, smaller cross beams, or even wires **5** to provide support for plants.

2

4

3

5

DECKING

DECK STYLES

There are basically two types of deck (if you don't include well-made decks and the badly-made variety!).

low-level decks

These are usually the easiest type to build as they are often laid onto roughly levelled ground and there is less digging and foundation work to do than with stone- or brick-covered areas. You can arrange the planks in many ways. The simplest is laid straight and butting up to each other **1** as with floors indoors, but you can use your imagination if you really want to be different. Laying the boards at an angle of 45 degrees looks impressive, but once started is no more difficult than laying the boards straight (see page 68). Even a small balcony **2** or roof terrace could benefit from decking as it is much lighter than stone.

To speed things up, you can also buy your decking as ready-made squares, either straight **3** or patterned. The rules for laying these are the same as planks: you need the same base frame, but the execution is much faster!

1

2

there are basically two types of deck (if you don't include the well-made and the badly-made variety)

3

4

raised decks

These are decks 600mm (2ft) or more above ground level, and if large in area, a structural engineer may need to be consulted to calculate the deck's load-bearing requirements and dimensions. Once you have decided the appropriate dimensions of the wood needed and the distance between supports, the construction is similar to low-level decks. Try to incorporate some steps, also made from timber **4**. Simple foundations are essential to support and secure raised decks.

👍 **TOMMY'S TIP For raised decks, a hand rail is essential. It should usually be 1.2m (4ft) above the deck to prevent people falling, without blocking the view. Vertical spindles (balusters) can be fitted where there are children. The spindles must be spaced no wider than 100mm (4in) centres to prevent children getting their heads stuck between them!**

CHOOSING YOUR WOOD

Wood makes an excellent flooring material when used properly. It's a natural, warm material and good-quality, well-preserved wood can last for many years. The main enemy of any timber structure is rotting; this is especially true of decks, as they are often on, or close to, the soil. If a suitable timber is not chosen, or it is not well protected, your deck will last only about five years.

Pressure-treated softwood, where the preservative has penetrated deep into the wood, is most commonly used. You can also use much more expensive, naturally decay-resistant wood, such as teak, western red cedar and oak, especially if the oak is green (unseasoned).

With all types of decking, slight gaps should be left between the boards to help drainage and increase air movement, which keeps the boards drier and so less prone to rotting.

THE FINISHING TOUCHES

1

2

3

4

OUTDOOR LIVING

With all the functions a modern garden has to perform, it is still possible to stamp your own character on it, even if you buy many of the items for the garden rather than make them yourself. If you enjoy summer evenings outdoors **1**, you can install some garden lighting to illuminate your patio **2** or highlight specific plants **3** and garden **4**. For me, comfortable furniture is a must. If you are going to relax, the best place to do it is in the garden with a glass in your hand, in an attractive chair **5**. Otherwise, simply make sure you have a place in the

5

6

8

7

garden where you can sit and dream **6**. Additions to the patio such as a lit pool **7** or a fountain or water feature **8** – within easy viewing of the seating area – will also help to make you feel relaxed.

USING THE SPACE

Having a small garden need not be a problem – see it as a challenge. If you do not have the space to spread out, you can always garden upwards, growing climbing plants, or hang baskets from the wall or fences. These areas are all part of your garden, so use them if you possibly can.

WATER FEATURES

Gardens and water go together naturally, and the logical progression for many keen gardeners is to add a water feature to satisfy the desire to have water in the garden as an attraction, rather than just to keep plants alive and growing.

The addition of a water feature to any garden instantly introduces a new dimension, since it immediately increases the range of plants that can be grown. It also creates an environment that will attract animals, birds and insects, and gives a feeling of being closer to nature, as well as (hopefully) controlling pests naturally. The presence of water can bring life and energy to the garden by providing movement and sound, and where a fountain is installed, visual attraction.

The controlled movement of artificially running water **1**, created by bubble springs, fountains, water jets and waterfalls, can create movement and activity previously lacking from an area of the garden. Coupled with this is the sound and atmosphere moving water can provide.

Not every garden is large enough to have a full-sized pond, but it is still possible to have a water feature on a smaller scale **2**. Ponds are not always practical in a garden anyway, particularly where there are young children because their natural curiosity always seems to draw them to the water. Even a depth of just a few inches of water is enough for a toddler to drown. However, it is possible to have an easy-to-build water feature that is perfectly safe, with even very young children playing in the garden. So you can still enjoy sound and movement from water without the extra work that a pond would involve.

Bubble fountains occupy an area as small as 300mm x 300mm (12in x 12in), with all of the workings and equipment totally hidden from view. They allow the water to rise up from nowhere and tumble over the stones before vanishing again.

1

2

outdoor landscaping

This is probably what I'm most known for, and I have a favourite – natural stone. If planned well, a mixture of different surfaces will complement each other, so you benefit from the best of both!

making patios & paths

It's funny how jobs which look quite complicated are often just the opposite. Laying slabs can be child's play if you just take your time and follow each step in a logical sequence. Once you have finished, there is no greater feeling than sweeping away the dust, setting out the garden furniture and opening a nice cool beer.

LAYING SLABS

First prepare your foundations (see page 34). Set out your slabs to check your layout and that you really have calculated properly! (see chart page 32). Position the first slab in a corner and work out in one direction. Use ready-made spacers (or small wooden pegs of about pencil thickness) between the slabs to keep the joints matching **1**.

MORTARING THE SLABS

After positioning the slabs, start by spreading a layer (bed) of mortar about 50mm (2in) thick (see page 36). Do a small section at a time over the sub-base, creating ridges in the mortar bed **2** so that the mortar can move and spread when the slab is tapped into position. Wet the undersides of the slabs before they are laid for better bonding.

Lay the first row of slabs to the line, checking that each slab is bedded into place in line with the string, at the desired level. Use your trowel between the slabs to gently ease them **3**. Any slab which rocks or tilts should be lifted, more mortar added and if necessary the slab re-laid. Use a rubber-headed hammer (or club hammer on a block of wood) to lightly tap each slab down into place until it is level with the string line. Then set up the two end slabs in the next line, and repeat the process for each line.

1

2

3

TOMMY'S ADVICE

As you lay the slabs, it is important to keep checking levels. Each slab needs to be level itself, but also level with the slabs surrounding it. This is particularly the case if the slabs are of different thickness or have a 'natural' textured finish on the top surface, as you can't easily see a change in level just by looking at them. Always check across both diagonals to ensure the slab is level in all directions. A gentle tap here and there should be enough to set things right and put you on the way to completing the perfect job.

👍 **TOP TIP** If you use a wet mortar mix for pointing the slabs, it will result in some unsightly staining on the surface of the slabs. I water the joints first and leave them to dry for an hour before adding a dry mixture of 3 parts soft sand and 1 part cement (see page 36).

4   **5**   **6**

JOINT FILLING (POINTING)

This is done to keep the paved area weather-proof and to help prevent weeds growing between the joints. Gently water the joints first with a watering can. Fill the joints between the slabs, pushing the mixture of sand and cement (see top tip) into the joints with a small trowel **4**. Run a ready-made jointing tool or a piece of bent copper pipe along the joints until the mixture is firmly packed into the joints, the water from the joint is drawn up by the dry mix to create a wet mortar joint without staining the slab **5**.

Brush away any surplus mortar mix from the surface of the slabs **6**, and leave until the mixture gradually sets, sealing the joints. A shoulder of mortar (haunching) can be laid along the outer edges of the paving to act as a anchor.

BLOCK PAVIORS/FLEXIBLE PAVING

Block paving is often referred to as 'flexible' paving, although the blocks don't feel flexible when you kneel on them to work. The individual blocks or bricks are laid on a base (bed) of dry sharp sand and bedded into position. This gives a strong, firm path but with a degree of movement, rather than being as rigid as materials like concrete. This flexible type of construction has become very popular for making garden patios and paths for a number of reasons:

• They are easy to lay (even for a newcomer to garden construction)

• They can be lifted and re-laid or re-used if you change your mind about the shape and style of the patio

• Your patio is much easier to repair if the odd unit within the patio becomes damaged or broken.

There are a number of different materials that can be used to make these paths, including traditional style bricks. These were often used in the past and can make a very attractive path, but be sure you use good-quality bricks, as the poorer quality ones are often damaged by frost. Concrete block paviors are made from a cement-based mixture which makes them fairly hard-wearing and frost-resistant, so they will probably last you for years. If you are not sure how things will fit or look, do a 'dry run' and lay out some paviors to see how the edges and pattern work, and how much cutting may need to be done. This avoids the embarrassment of running out of materials – especially if someone is watching you work.

LAYING BLOCK PAVIORS

After the foundations have been prepared (see page 34), string out a line to mark the position and fall of your first row of paviors. Complete the edges before starting on the middle. Fill the area inside the brick edging with sharp sand **1**. This should be to a level about halfway up the sides of the brick edging. Compact the sand with a piece of wood

1

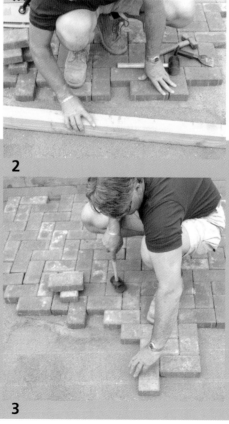

2

3

4

5

6

7

2, a rammer or vibrating plate compactor (Wacker) until the level is sufficient to hold the paviors about 6mm (¼in) above the intended height of the finished patio. Bed the inner blocks onto the sand to fill the area with the pattern you have chosen **3**, laying whole paviors first before cutting sections of pavior to fill in the gaps as dictated by your pattern. Make sure that the paviors butt up to one another with no gaps between them. Stand on the paved surface as you go, if you are light (unlike me) you can work from a plank or board to spread your weight. Bed in the blocks using a soft mallet **4**. After the outer layer of paviors has been completed, place a shoulder or 'haunching' along the outside to prevent them spreading outwards away from the patio.

Once the paviors are firm, and the area is finished, cut open a bag of special block paving sand **5**, which is very fine and must be totally dry. Spread this layer over the paviors and sweep it to fill in the spaces **6**. A vibrating plate compactor (Wacker) can be used to compact the paviors and vibrate the kiln-dried sand in between, locking the whole thing together **7**. Beware, this machine packs quite a punch and can easily get away from you! On a smaller area, tap the paviors down with a lump hammer, using a piece of wooden board to avoid marking or breaking the blocks; this can act as a prehistoric compactor plate!

TOMMY'S ADVICE

Whatever pattern you decide on, it will mean that some paviors will have to be cut to size by placing them on a firm base, then using a lump hammer and broad, flat 'bolster' chisel. If you have to cut many blocks, you should hire a block cutting machine, which looks like a heavy-duty guillotine – and works like one, so keep your fingers out of the way if you still want to count up to ten!

STONE, AND BRICK PATHS

After concrete, stone and bricks are probably the most popular materials for making a path. Stone slabs are slightly ahead, mind you, as it is possible to cover an area more quickly, making you feel that you really have achieved something.

As with other types of path, the surface is only as good as the effort put into the foundations below it (see page 34) – skimp on that and your path will settle and break up, making it a high-risk obstacle course. Bricks, blocks or stone setts would be preferable for a path that is curved, as smaller sized units can be arranged to cope with the curves **1**, while stone slabs might need cutting. The aim should be to have the path's finished surface level with, or slightly higher than, the surrounding soil, but slightly below the level of the lawn, allowing easy mowing and no trimming. Spread a layer (bed) of mortar

about 50mm (2in) thick, creating ridges in the mortar bed **2**. Perk up a simple stone slab path by leaving larger gaps between the slabs and inserting gravel or small stones in wet mortar **3**. Once completed, you have a very different path! **4**

1

4

GRAVEL PATHS

6

5

GRAVEL PATHS

Possibly the easiest way to create a new path is to lay down gravel – but it is not as simple as just up-ending a few bags. Unless it is laid properly, a walk along a gravel path can seem like jogging in treacle as your feet sink down among the pebbles. The best way to produce a

hard-wearing gravel path with a good-quality finish is to prepare a firm base and use clean pea gravel or crushed stone 10–20mm (⅜–¾in) in diameter. Gravel is quick and easy to lay (though it is hard work to move about) and relatively inexpensive when compared to other materials. It is also an excellent burglar deterrent – not even an Apache could sneak over gravel without being heard.

Gravel paths work well in a shaded garden where the light levels are low, because the pale colour reflects the available light. Gravel is a great solution where a curved, meandering path is desired, as there is none of the time-consuming stone or brick cutting associated with other surfaces **5**. On the down-side, a gravel path tends to spread, and some sort of fixed edging will be needed to keep the gravel from spreading into lawns and flower beds. In order to look good, a gravel path also needs raking regularly.

Alternatively, you could use self-binding gravel, which is crushed stone consisting of particles varying in size from 2 to 15mm (⅛ to ⅝in) and, because of the mixture of particle sizes, it binds together naturally when wetted and compacted to form a firm, long-lasting surface **6**.

decking

Decking is a great way of building a patio or outdoor seating and dining area quickly – also you get a free sawdust mulch to cover your garden and off-cuts to start your barbecue.

LAYING DECKING

DECKING FOUNDATIONS

Fungus is the main enemy of wood – the sort that is found in the soil, often millions of spores in a single cupful. To reduce the chance of this rot affecting the wood, the deck should be laid onto a foundation that prevents the wood touching the soil.

Decking is a very quick and easy way to cover an old concrete or paved patio. Rather than breaking up the old surface, use it to form the foundation of the new deck. Alternatively, dig out the soil to the required depth and set brick or concrete pads into the ground.

You need a prepared base of concrete pads, bricks or blocks set into the ground at regular intervals of about 1.5m (5ft) to carry the load-bearing supports or 'joists' **1**. With foundation pads at these spacings, joists with a minimum size of 100 x 50mm (4 x 2in) are needed to form the deck base. I always use timber no smaller than 100 x 50mm (6 x 2in) to make the base. The joists are set at right angles to the deck boards – and on a slightly uneven site, any correction to the level is usually made to the foundations.

After setting the blocks in place, check at regular intervals to ensure that they are level, using a plank and spirit level **2**. Packing under the blocks or pads with mortar or spare pieces of wood will help adjust to the correct level.

Before the decking frame is set out on the foundation pads, you can lay sections of felt or damp-proof course onto the pads **3**. This waterproof layer will help check moisture rising up from the ground and prevent it entering the wood.

1

2

3

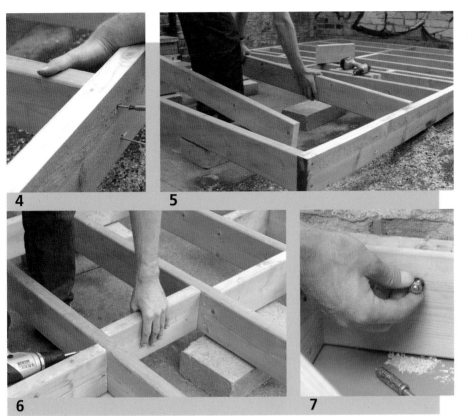

4 **5**

6 **7**

Where a deck is intended to be adjacent to a house or other building, it is possible to take full advantage of this structure to provide stability for the deck itself, although care must always be taken not to interfere with the damp-proof course of the building. This situation is ideal where the decked area is intended to become an 'outdoor' room or open-air extension of the house.

The deck is bolted to the wall using expanding masonry bolts fitted into holes drilled into the wall at the appropriate level, according to whether a low-level or raised deck is

MAKING THE FRAME

Measure and cut the lengths of timber to make the decking frame (see page 33). This will form the outer support for the entire deck. Drill two holes with a 6mm (⅝in) drill at diagonally opposite corners 25mm (1in) from the end. Fasten the joints with 75mm (3in) screws. To check that the frame is square, measure across diagonal corners; if the frame is square, these two measurements should be identical. Cut the support joists to length. Mark the position of each joist on the decking frame, drill two holes through the frame, then fasten the joists to the frame to make a butt joint using 75mm (3in) decking screws **4**. Space the joists at 400mm (16in) centres across the frame **5**. Make sure that they are level. Now add the transverse bracing timbers (noggins) **6**.

Decking fitted onto an existing building can not only provide a hard surface, and if the right type of wood is used or a suitably-coloured treatment is chosen and applied, the deck can complement it too.

desired. Where the deck adjoins the wall, attach a sound timber wall plate to the wall with substantial masonry fixing bolts **7**. This provides the major structural support for the deck. The drilled holes can be filled with resin, and bolts can be fitted into the holes, while the resin is still wet. Before mounting the wall plate, cut notches nto

TOMMY'S ADVICE

Where you build a deck against the wall of your house or other building, remember to leave a space in the decking frame to avoid covering air bricks or vents. Blocking such vents can lead to problems with dampness or moulds on the walls in later years.

8

9

10

11

12

13

TOMMY'S ADVICE

A quick way to ensure a 45-degree angle is to use your garden saw. The plastic handle will usually incorporate a 45-degree angle on the toothed edge which you can measure against by holding a straight-edge along it – and you thought it was just a pretty handle!

into the top edge, to accommodate the ends of the supporting joists.

In this project, the decking timbers are being laid at a 45-degree angle, rather than the normal square 90-degree pattern, so you will need to mark out (at 45-degrees) where to start on the framework. To save timber, it is best to measure the longest piece **8** and then mark the first angle on the frame **9**. Once you have that in place it should be plain sailing. Start to lay out the decking boards and drill and countersink the screw holes before fixing them into position with decking screws. You will need two screws per board, per joist, set 19mm (¾in) in from the edges. Work systematically across the deck area, leaving a space of about 10mm (⅜in) between individual boards.

14

👍 **TOP TIP** To make sure that the deck boards are evenly spaced, use small pieces of wood (about 10mm/⅜in wide), screwdrivers **10,** or even manufactured spacer wedges to speed thing up **11**.

It's a good idea to run a string line over the top of the joists to make sure you are drilling through the deck boards at the correct place **12**. Pre-drill the deck boards before fixing them.

Finish the deck by cutting away any surplus sections of boards where they overlap the outer edges of the frame. Clamping a section of surplus board close to the outer edge of the deck to use as a guide for the saw **13** is a good way of making sure that you get a clean, even cut along the edge **14**. Fix boards to the outside 'facing edges' of the deck to conceal the framework and joints.

TOMMY'S ADVICE

For larger deck areas, it is more convenient to build several sections of decking and place them together. Because you are unlikely to find support timbers long enough, this can make assembly and construction much easier, especially where a deck is on two or more levels. Also, if any valuable items, such as jewellery, drop between the decking boards, one section can be lifted to retrieve the item without ripping up the whole deck.

lawns

If an Englishman's home is his castle, his lawn is his garden grindstone. The better you look after your lawn, the more work it seems to need: scarifying, mowing, spiking, watering and raking. It seems that if you have a lawn – unless the garden will be used by children and dogs – only a snooker table surface and texture will do for many people.

THE LIVING CARPET

For general garden use, grass is a brilliant surface – and it is so many things to so many different gardeners. As a plant, it is fairly easy to grow. Keep it fed and watered and you will have a passable lawn. Put in the care and attention and you will have the perfect foil for all the other plants in your garden. It is also relatively hard wearing, able to withstand both drought and heavy rain as well as being constantly walked over – and a playing surface for games throughout the year. For the less energetic, the same surface is just as good for lounging on or sunbathing – so far we have yet to find a more durable ground cover for general garden use.

MAKING A LAWN

You could call this carpet laying for gardeners. Using lawn in this way is not as new as you might think. Cutting, moving and re-laying turf is an ancient practice,

and was most often used as an effective insulating and weather-proofing material for the roofs of houses. This use is less common now – possibly due to the shorter lengths of cable supplied with modern electric mowers!

Although turf is seen as the 'quick fix' instant lawn, it involves as much work as seed lawns – the only real advantage is that you get a more quickly established lawn.

PREPARATION

Rake the soil roughly level with a fine rake, breaking it down to a fine texture, and smoothing out bumps and hollows **1**. A base dressing of fertilizer, at between 150–200 grams per square metre (4–6 ounces per square yard), can be added at this stage. Using a gravel board is a very easy way to smooth out the humps and hollows, especially while the soil surface is still loose **2**. A water-filled roller is ideal for firming the soil after it has been

1   2   3   4

5   6   7

TOMMY'S ADVICE

Turf has to be laid within about three days of delivery or it will deteriorate. The grass quickly turns to compost due to heat and moisture being generated while it is stacked in rolls.

levelled, and it will also expose any remaining soft areas of soil **3**, but do not use it for levelling the lawn once laid. Firm the ground by walking over it in a shuffling motion, taking short steps and applying pressure with your heels **4**. This will firm the soil without compacting it. Rake over the soil again, bringing it to a fine tilth.

LAYING TURF

After preparing the site, mark out the lawn edge, using a wooden plank or garden line for straight edges **5**. Lay the turves on at least two edges of the lawn area, working out from a corner if possible, across the plot. Open each roll of turf, pressing it firmly into place against the preceding one **6**. Always use kneel-on boards when laying the turf, never walk on it **7**. Push the turves close together to close up any gaps or joints, but arrange them so that the joints are not in line. Where two pieces meet, tuck them in tightly – so that the two pieces of turf fit snugly. Once all of the turf has been laid, sweep it with a stiff brush to lift the flattened grass and remove any loose stones and dirt. If necessary, water the area thoroughly.

👍 **TOP TIP When laying turf, work in a forward direction, and lay a plank on the row of turves that have just been laid. This firms the turf into position as you work and saves an extra job.**

If you are laying turf in dry weather, water regularly and check the turves after about two to three days. If they have started to shrink, you will need to push them together again and give the lawn a good watering. Never walk on your lawn while there is frost on it, your footprints will damage the grass, leaving brown 'footprints' for several weeks.

MAKING A LAWN FROM SEED – FEEDING THE BIRDS

1
2
3

The best time for sowing a lawn is when the soil is warm and moist enough for quick germination and rapid growth of the grass seedlings. However, if you're like me, you will probably just do it when you get the time!

PREPARATION

Rake the soil roughly level with a fine rake, breaking it down to a fine texture, and smoothing out bumps and hollows. Prepare the ground by walking on it with your heels close together **1**. Add a base dressing of fertilizer, at between 150 to 200 grams per square metre (4 to 6 ounces per square yard). As a guide to help you sow the seed more evenly, mark the area into equal 1m (1yd) squares using canes and garden line **2**.

SOWING

Sow grass seed when the soil is dry on the surface but moist beneath, otherwise you will pick up most of the seed on your boots as you walk over the ground. Weigh enough seed for each area as given on the pack, and sow at about knee height to allow the seed to disperse evenly. After

sowing, lightly rake the soil with a fine rake in different directions **3**. This will cover the seed and ensure it comes into contact with the moist soil.

👍 **TOP TIP Save time by marking out a single 1sq. m (1sq. yd) area. Measure the seed according to the instructions, put it into a cup and sow this correct measure to give a visual reference of the required density 4.**

4

children's play areas

In an ideal world and if your garden is large enough, your kids would prefer their own separate area where they can play. Of course, once they start playing they will probably take over the rest of the garden anyway.

PLAY EQUIPMENT

Inevitably, many of the games played will involve a degree of rough-and-tumble, so any play equipment should be checked for sharp edges, or any place where limbs or fingers may get trapped and injured. Also, the surfaces on which the children play must have some give in them, to reduce the chance of injury when falling or landing.

For small children, sand is a popular material, but for playing in rather than running over or landing on. Always make any 'soft landing' areas quite large; there is no point in having a soft surface if it is too small and there is a risk of a child landing on the retaining edge of the area and getting injured.

Shredded bark is very popular as a soft surface to land on while playing, and is a perfect material beneath swings or slides, where a bumpy landing is inevitable at the bottom of the slide. You need to put down a layer of weed-suppressing fabric before putting down the shredded bark **1**. A depth of at least 100–150mm (4–6in) of shredded bark will be required to cushion a fall and help with a soft landing.

1

👍 **TOP TIP Where sand is used to provide a surface, playgrade washed sand is the best, as it will not stain skin or clothing. Make sure that it can be covered when not in use, as many unsavoury items can get buried in it.**

raised areas/beds

Raised beds are a great way to garden. Instead of having to stoop down or get on your knees to work, the garden is raised up to a convenient level for the gardener – no more stooping or bending. Raised beds also give you more surface area of garden: you can grow plants down the sides of the bed as well as in it.

RAISED BEDS

When faced with a new garden, it is often an instinctive reaction to start moving earth about and trying to create a level garden – or at least reduce the angle of any slope within the garden. While this may be desirable for a lawn or seating area, it is not always essential for the rest of the garden to be level – in fact, there are few garden features that need perfectly level ground.

1

WORK WITH THE SLOPE

Gardens built on steeper slopes can be made much more interesting by working with the slope, rather than trying to fight it and move vast quantities of earth. Terraces, held in place with retaining walls built using durable materials, can be used to create a split-level garden of two (or more) separate heights, giving separate sections of level garden space, rather than trying to make the whole garden function on one level **1**.

work with a slope rather than fighting it

Access can be provided by steps, a sloping pathway, or a combination of the two, in designs which can be as ornamental as your imagination will allow. In steeply-sloping gardens, a series of winding, gradually-sloping paths not only provide easier and more gentle access, but can help to create the illusion that the garden is larger than it really is.

Retaining walls need not be used exclusively in a sloping garden, they are often put to very good use on flat sites, where the level varies hardly at all. In this instance, the wall can be used to add height and interest to the garden by providing an extra dimension.

MATERIALS FOR RAISED BEDS

The most common and strongest materials to use are probably brick **2** or stone. But don't be deterred if you don't feel up to bricklaying. You can use wood cut

2 **3** **4** **5**

specially in blocks and laid like bricks **3**. These are simply nailed together, but some are put together with plastic dowels – a bit like Lego really (see page 80). The use of railway sleepers has been discouraged, which is a shame since because of their weight they offer the simplest way to build a bed. But don't despair, you can now buy concrete sleepers with a wood texture and I would defy you to tell the difference. They are a cinch to build with (except for the weight) and you can achieve a simple bed or wall in no time. They can be used either horizontally **4** or vertically **5** and even as a surface.

FILLING RAISED BEDS

Creating a raised bed can open up a whole range of possibilities when gardening on a level site, as it is possible to isolate the soil or compost held within the bed. This allows you to increase the range of plants that can be grown in the garden.

A raised bed filled with ericaceous compost or acidic soil makes it possible to grow plants such as camellias and rhododendrons in gardens where the soil has a high lime content, particularly if the soil in the raised bed does not come into contact with the soil below. Plants such as alpines prefer a dry, free-draining soil, and can be grown in raised beds built above the natural soil as long as plenty of grit is added. The other advantage here is that it is much easier to view small alpine plants if they are raised above ground level.

Where raised beds are used for plants such as vegetables, or plants with no special requirements, it is better to half-fill the bed with good soil or compost. Dig this in to mix it with the garden soil below, before filling the top layers of the bed with more soil or compost. This mixing of new soil with the native soil is important to establish a link between the different materials so that they dry out and absorb water at approximately the same rate. If the plants being grown in the raised bed need very free-draining conditions, sand or gravel can be mixed with the compost to increase the drainage rate of the soil in the bed.

MAKING A BRICK-RAISED BED

Low walls are quite easy to build with a little practice, and although it would take many years to achieve bricklayers' standards and speed, a small wall can be built with care and planning. If you have not laid bricks before, it is a good idea to dry-lay the first course on the foundation strip with a 12mm (½in) gap between each. Where the wall is a single brick thick, it will need additional strengthening if it is to reach a height of more than 450mm (18in). This can be provided by upright columns (piers) incorporated into a run of a single-brick wall at intervals of about 3m (9½ft). Each pier needs to be a minimum of twice the thickness of the wall it is supporting.

The really hard work comes with digging a foundation. For a small raised bed up to 450mm (18in) high, you will need a concrete strip foundation a minimum of 150mm (6in) thick and at least twice the width of the wall, laid on compacted soil. If you are careful and get the levels right at this stage, it makes bricklaying much easier.

MAKING THE BED

To keep the wall straight, set up a string line along the length of the wall. Using a bricklayer's trowel, spread a bed of mortar **1** on the concrete foundation, ready to receive the first course of bricks, and set the first brick in place with its face in line with the string line. Check that this brick is level using a spirit level. Using a bricklayer's trowel, butter some mortar onto one end of the second brick **2** and set it in place, butting it up to touch the first brick, sandwiching the mortar between them. Gently tap each brick into place with the trowel handle **3**.

👍 **TOP TIP Leave some of the joints open (no mortar in them) on the bottom course of the wall 4, this will allow water to drain out of the bed and prevent waterlogging.**

Starting at a corner, lay the second course of bricks with the joints overlapping those on the first course – a simple overlap, known as stretcher bond **5**. Check your wall is level **6** and vertical as each course is laid. Where half bricks are needed, cut them using a broad-bladed 'bolster' chisel and a lump hammer. Chop a line into each face of the brick to get a clean break.

The final or top course of the wall can be of concrete or stone coping to provide an ornamental finish and keep the weather out. Have the mortar slightly stiff so that it is not squeezed out of the joints. Once this has been laid, allow the mortar joints to dry for about 30 minutes before running a piece of hose along the joints (see page 14), or rubbing with a jointer. Finally, carefully dust over with a stiff hand broom to remove any unwanted mortar.

MAKING A BENCH-RAISED BED

A raised bed can be almost any length and, within reason, any height, but the width of the bed is important. The ideal width is 1.5–2m (5–6ft), so that it is possible to reach the centre of the bed from each side. The bed we are making here measures 1.2 x 3m (4 x 10ft), but the dimensions can be easily altered to suit your garden space.

One very simple and useful way of increasing the structural strength of a raised bed is to add a broad wooden capping to tie the sides together. This also has another very functional benefit, as it forms a seat around the rim of the bed and allows you to garden sitting down. This bed is made for siting directly on a flat surface.

Start by cutting all of the timber to length, including the sides, ends, corner posts, side posts and end caps.

Cut the sides from exterior grade plywood to the height required, about 300mm (12in) and screw the four sides together. Check they are square and level.

Cut 6 sections of 100 x 100 x 300mm (4 x 4 x 12in) for support posts. Fix the low sides together with a support post in each corner (on the inside) with screws to make a rectangular box, and check to make sure they are square and level **1**. Attach the two remaining support posts to the sides of the box (in the middle) but position them on the outer surface with 90mm (3½in) screws **2**. Cut five pieces of 50 x 200mm (2 x 8in) to a length of 200mm (8in), next cut these pieces again, diagonally, to make ten triangles. Fix one of these triangle braces to each middle support post with screws **3**. Attach the remaining triangles to the outsides of the box, close to the corner posts. These will act as extra support for the bench seat **4**. Cut four lengths of 50 x 200mm (2 x 8in) timber to form the bench seat to fit over the sides and ends of the box; use one as a template for the 45-degree mitred corners **5**. Position the sections of bench seat and secure them in place by driving screws through the bench into the triangle braces. Sand the edges of the bench boards until they are smooth **6**.

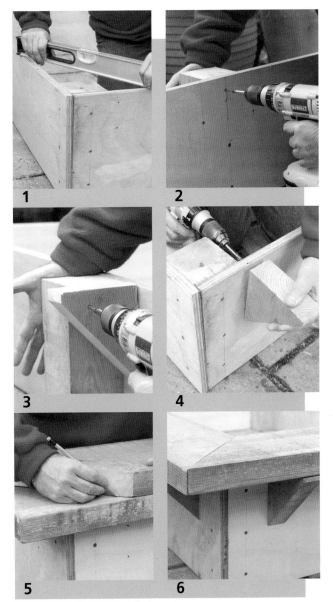

1 2 3 4 5 6

👍 **TOP TIP** Mark and drill the ends of the side and end boards for the screws that will attach them to the corner posts. Then fix the two side boards together with a 'G' clamp and drill holes through both at once to guarantee that the sets of holes are in identical positions. Repeat the process with the end boards.

MAKING A RAISED BED FROM A READY-MADE SYSTEM

Raised beds provide a neat gardening area, where it is possible to garden without having to stoop or bend too much. Here, we are using a system of interlocking wooden blocks called WoodBlocX, to make a bed that is easily built with these standard units. And provided the walls are kept square and level, this is the perfect system for the DIY gardener.

Lay out the WoodBlocX in the correct positions. Use the longer blocks for the sides and ends and the shorter blocks around the corners so that they will key together like bricks to create a low wooden wall for the planting bed. The first layer of the wall should have ground spikes driven through the holes to anchor the blocks into the soil.

Assemble the wedges and dowels and drive them into the middle and end holes in the first row. Fit the second layer on top, driving down onto the dowels and wedges to lock them into place **1**, so that the wall can be built up in layers. Repeat this process when adding each layer.

For each corner, fit a metal angle plate over the holes in the corner WoodBlocX **2**, and drive dowels through to

4

key the corner joints together **3**. Check the corners with a square to make sure the angles are correct. Repeat this process at each corner.

A top layer of capping can be fitted to the wall. Cut off the top three notches in the dowel protruding from

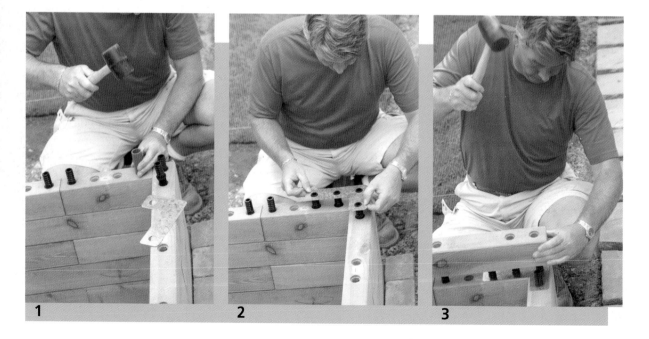

1   2   3

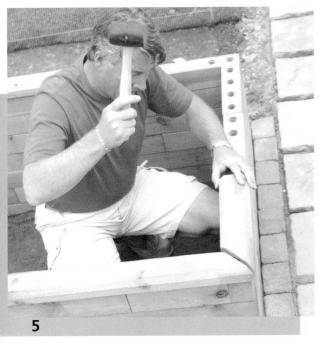

5

the wall **4**. Start at a corner with the pre-cut mitred ends touching **5**, and work towards the centre of each wall section. If you need to cut any sections of capping, make the cuts to coincide with a point between the dowels so that the ends are secure. Finally, you are ready to plant **6**.

👍 **TOP TIP** When building the walls, stagger the vertical joints along the wall and overlap the corner joints to allow them to key together so avoiding weak spots.

6

raised areas/steps

The main function for any set or flight of steps is to form a link between two or more levels, making access from one part of the garden to another much easier. To do this well, the steps need to fit in with their surroundings so that they also act as a visual link.

BRICK & STONE STEPS

The steeper the slope in a garden, the more likely it is that you will want to make some steps to get up to the high point without too much effort. Going up there is the problem – gravity will always help you get back down. On a sloping site, most steps are 'cut-in' – so called because they are cut into the slope. The most common type of step you are likely to see in a garden is one with the front, or riser, made from bricks, with the flat surface made from stone or concrete slabs. Steps can be made from all the usual materials, including solid stone **1**, stone with brick risers **2**, slate **3**, slate paddlestones **4**, wood **5**, metal **6**, and even decking **7**.

1

2

3

4

5

6

7

BUILDING RUSTIC STEPS

1

2

3

If you want a more rustic setting for a slope, rather than building steps using brick or stone, you can use wood, which will quickly blend into the surroundings. Of course, the other bonuses are that wood is much easier to lug up the slope and is much easier to work with, so you can get the job done quickly.

MEASURING AND MARKING STEPS

Knock a length of batten into the ground at the base of the slope and cut off the top level with the top of the slope. Measure the height of the batten and divide it by 150mm (6in) to give you the number of steps you need. Now measure from the top of the batten to the top of the slope **1**, and divide this figure by 300–450mm (12–18in) to give you the size of each step. The steps can then be marked out on the ground with pegs and string or spray paint.

Start by marking out and cutting your steps into the slope, working from the bottom upwards. Each step has two short logs about 800–900mm (3–5in) in diameter to form the risers of the steps. Just in front of these logs position two more with pointed-tips about 100mm (4in) in from the ends of the risers. Drive these logs into the ground so that they are about 50mm (2in) below the top of the top riser log **2**.

4

5

Stack the two riser logs on top of one another, pushing them firmly against the stakes **3**, and place one or two spades full of soil on the uphill side of the logs to hold them in position. Continue up the slope, repeating this process until you reach the top.

Finally, back-fill each step with soil and scalpings and compact it until it is about 50mm (2in) below the top of the riser log **4**, before adding a layer of gravel **5** to bring the filling up level with the riser logs.

outdoor boundaries

I have witnessed terrible feuds between neighbours over the years, most of them over boundaries! So consult your neighbours regarding your proposals, in order to avoid your own 'Gunfight at the not OK corral'!

erecting wooden fences

With so many types and styles of fencing available, it can be difficult to decide which is right for you. Select a fence that fits in with both the surroundings and your garden, making it decorative as well as functional, if possible. Of course, your choice of fencing may depend on how nosy you think your neighbours are!

ERECTING A CLOSE-BOARDED FENCE

It is important to mark out the intended line of the fence before any holes are dug, to help keep the line straight and to make sure the fence is erected along its intended route. The type of fence will dictate whether all of the posts are erected first or one at a time along with the other fencing components. For example, when erecting a

TOP TIP Cut a piece of batten or bamboo cane to the equivalent length of one post plus one panel to make a template for measuring the distance at which the holes should be dug for each post.

fence made from prefabricated panels, fix the posts as you erect the fence, so that the entire fence is built by erecting panels and posts alternately.

It is advisable to bury one quarter of each post, to provide a firm foundation and help the fence withstand windy conditions. For example, for a 1.8m (6ft) high fence, dig a 600mm (2ft) hole to take a 2.4m (8ft) post. Where possible, adjust the spacing of the posts in order to avoid obstructions such as large tree roots or concrete left in from previous posts.

For posts that have to be inserted across a paved patio, lift enough slabs to dig the holes. It may be necessary to

break up sections of concrete foundations beneath the slabs to obtain sufficient depth to accommodate the posts. As an alternative, it is possible to buy post 'sockets', which can be bolted into holes drilled into the patio and fitted with expanding bolts. Provided a firm anchorage can be obtained, these metal sockets will do an adequate job, although the fittings are often visible.

ERECTING THE FENCE

The cladding for a close-boarded fence is erected on site, but the support materials, such as posts and horizontal arris rails, are usually pre-cut to make construction easier and quicker. These parts are usually fitted together with flanged arris rail brackets that hold the arris rails in place at set points on the upright posts. The cladding for the fence is made from feather-edged boards 100–150mm (4–6in) wide and 16mm (⅝in) thick on one edge and tapering to 3mm (⅛in) on the other.

1   2

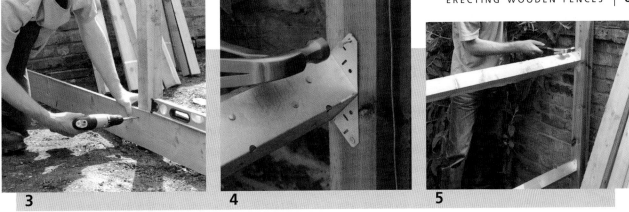

3 4 5

Start by stringing out a line to mark the intended route of the fence. Knock a peg into the ground at each end of the intended line of the fence and stretch a marker line between the two points **1**.

Mark out the positions for the posts at pre-determined intervals (see top tip opposite). Using a spade, dig a hole at least a spade's width across and dig down to the required depth **2**. When you have reached a sufficient depth, taper the sides of the hole slightly so that you can pack hardcore and concrete around the post. Follow the instructions for putting in a wooden post on page 23.

You need to use wooden gravel boards that fit at the base of the fence so that the featherboards do not come into contact with the damp ground; this will prevent them rotting. Screw the gravel boards to the bottoms of the posts, using a spirit level to check that the levels are correct **3**. Mark the positions for the horizontal arris rails. One is usually positioned about 300mm (12in) above the gravel board and the upper one about 300mm (12in) below the top of the fence line. Fasten the brackets loosely to the posts **4**, before fitting the arris rails into the brackets, then fix the brackets firmly to the posts **5**.

With the framework in place you can start to attach the cladding. Each board is nailed to the top and bottom arris rails with a single ringnail **6** on the left-hand side. You need to overlap the boards by about 12mm (½in) so that as you fix each board the right-hand side of the previous board is trapped in position. Use a pre-cut spacer to check that the distance between the boards is the same, which makes the end result more pleasing to the eye **7**. Check the boards regularly with a spirit level to be sure they are vertical **8**.

6 7 8

BUILDING A FENCE WITH CONCRETE POSTS

Even though the wooden panels are more flimsy than the wooden posts that support them, it is usually the posts that deteriorate most quickly, often rotting at soil level. If you want a fence to last, it is well worth investing in a set of concrete posts that will last forever – or so it seems. The concrete posts have grooves on either side, so the fence is constructed using pre-fabricated panels that slot straight in. This reduces the number of clips or fittings you need to hold your fence in place.

Follow the basic rules on page 86 for measuring the site and digging the post holes. Ram a layer of hardcore (broken bricks or small stones) into the bottom of the hole to support the base of the post and provide drainage. Insert the post and position it in the hole. Pour loose hardcore into the hole around the post (if required, get someone to hold the post upright while you check with a spirit level that the post is vertical), and ram the hardcore firmly into position.

Ram more hardcore around the post, leaving a hole about 300mm (12in) deep to be filled with concrete.

Position each post in a hole and keep checking with a spirit level to ensure the posts are upright **1**. The quickest way to cement in your posts is to use a ready-made pack. This is probably more viable for a small garden than mixing up your own load. Each bag is enough for one hole, so you can't go wrong measuring it out. Add the dry post-fixing concrete to the hole **2**, tamping it down with the end of a piece of batten before adding water **3** (following the instructions on the bag). Allow the concrete to set sufficiently (about 30 minutes). Alternatively, mix some concrete to a firm consistency. Use a trowel or shovel to drop the concrete into the hole all round the post and tamp it down with the end of a batten. Either way, leave the concrete just below the surface, to allow soil to cover it and smooth it to slope away from the post.

1   2   3

4

TOMMY'S ADVICE

If your old fence post is sound but has rotted in the ground, you can shore it up by bracing the post above ground with a short concrete spur. You must remove the rotted stump by digging the soil from around it. Insert the spur, pack hardcore around it, and fill with concrete. The concrete posts come ready drilled for coach screws (screws with hexagonal heads). Drill through the wooden post and insert the screws. Use a socket spanner to draw the wooden post tightly against the spur **A**. Then re-fix the fence panel between the posts **B**.

A

Slot a concrete gravel board into the post. At the end of the gravel board, dig the hole for the second post. Lower the post into place and cement it in as before. After the concrete has set and the posts are firm, the fence panels can be lowered into position by lifting them up and sliding them down the grooves in the posts **4**. On exposed sites, it may be necessary to support a panel fence temporarily by wedging struts against the posts **5**.

Leave the concrete to harden for about a week before removing the struts.

👍 **TOP TIP Fitting the gravel boards and the fence panels is much easier with two people.**

5

B

BUILDING A FENCE USING METAL SPIKES

Instead of anchoring fence posts in concrete, you can plug the base of each post into the square socket of a metal spike driven into firm ground. Use a 600mm (2ft) spike for fences up to 1.2m (4ft) high, and a 750mm (2½ft) spike for a 1.8m (6ft) fence. This method is much quicker than digging holes and concreting the posts into position, but is not recommended for stony ground since it is difficult to drive the spikes in and keep them straight.

Start by knocking a peg into the ground at each end of the intended line of the fence and stretch a marker line between the two points (see page 86). Use a gravel board to measure between the posts.

Place a ready-made post driver in the socket or a scrap of hardwood post. This enables you to hammer the wooden post rather than the socket as you drive it into the ground, protecting the metal from crumpling. Drive the spike partly into the ground with a sledgehammer **1**. Use a spirit level held upright against the socket to make certain the spike is straight **2**. The post can twist as you push it into the ground, so adjust by twisting the metal arms of the the post driver **3**. Hammer the spike into the ground **4** until only the socket is visible.

The actual post can then be inserted into the socket and knocked into place with the sledgehammer. Secure by tightening the clamping bolts or by screwing through the side of the socket, depending on the type of spike **5**.

FINAL FINISHES

Fix the metal brackets to the centre of each upright post **6**, two brackets to each post, and slot the panel into the brackets **7**.

1

2

3

4

6

7

8

9

it will be easier
if you enlist
some help
sliding in the
panel

Seat the panel on a brick to hold it in place until you
have made sure it is the correct height and level before
fastening it to the brackets. Alternatively, the panels can
be fixed to the posts by hammering nails through from
the outer frame of the fence panel into the fence post
beyond. If the frame starts to split, blunt the nails by
tapping their points with a hammer. It will be easier if
you enlist some help to slide in the panel.

Finally, cut each post to length. Fix a string line and
use a spirit level all along the fence **8** to mark where to
cut the posts **9**. Leave about 50mm (2in) above the top
of the fence. If you are adding a trellis panel, save the
post cutting until after you
have fixed the trellis. Using
a circular saw, cut each
post **10** and to prevent the
wood from rotting, finish
off with a ready-made
wooden cap **11**. These are
treated and help to shed
water. You could also
chamfer the top with a
single or double bevel.

All fence panels and
posts are treated, but if
you want to personalize
your fence and bring some
colour into your garden,
there are many paint
products now available **12**.

5

10

11

12

trellis & screening

We often think of fences, trellises and the like as structures to erect along the boundary to establish our 'turf' and enclose our garden and property. But trellis, and natural screens especially, can also be used to grow plants on, and to act as dividers.

MAKING YOUR OWN TRELLIS

It's very easy to buy trellis, it comes in a range of sizes up to 1.8 x 1.8m (6 x 6ft). It is often a standard width but at heights of 300mm (12in), 600mm (24in) and 900mm (36in) as well as 1.2m (4ft) and 1.5m (5ft) just like panel fences. This is great if you have a standard size of garden, but you may face a situation where a standard size won't fit, and when this happens, it is easier to make your own. This also allows you to produce your own pattern.

Start by cutting lengths of timber battens to make an outside frame, either rectangular or square depending on the space you want to fill. Position the corners, checking that they are square **1**, then nail them in place. Now begin to build up the trelliswork by fastening the vertical battens. Start at one side of the frame and fasten the first batten in place to the top and bottom of the frame **2**. Work across the panel, adding battens and nailing them into place **3**.

Next, turn the panel over and start working from the bottom of the frame up to the top, adding battens at

TOP TIP Once you have decided how far apart the strips of batten are to be placed, cut spacers of the correct length and this will save you having to measure the distance every time you add a batten to the frame.

regular intervals positioned horizontally. As well as nailing these battens to the frame, additional nails can be added where the horizontal and vertical battens cross one another.

Finally, saw off any lengths of batten that are sticking out beyond the edges of the frame. Coat the trellis with wood preservative or a water-based paint.

1   2   3

PUTTING UP A REMOVEABLE TRELLIS SCREEN

Trellis is light, easy to handle and offers an almost limitless variety of design possibilities and options for the imaginative gardener. There are two factors to consider when fixing trellis against a vertical surface, such as a fence or wall. First, once the trellis is fitted and plants have started to grow through it, it is difficult to repair and maintain the trellis without damaging the plants. Second, it is difficult to repair and maintain the wall or fence without damaging the plants or the trellis supporting them.

One solution to these problems is to position the trellis about 300mm (12in) above ground level and hinge the lower edge to a wooden batten mounted on the vertical surface. It will then be possible to release the other fixings and allow the trellis to swing free of the wall, permitting access to carry out maintenance work behind it.

Prepare three timber battens for the top, middle and bottom. Hold the battens horizontally against the wall, starting about 300mm (12in) above ground level, and fix each of them to the wall with screws and plugs.

Screw three sets of hinges to a piece of trellis you have made earlier. Leaving the top of the trellis on the ground, lift the base of the piece until it is level with the lowest wall-mounted batten. Position the hinges on the front edge of the batten and screw them onto the batten **4**.

Pull up the trellis **5** and attach the trellis frame to the other battens on the wall. When you need to detach the trellis, simply unscrew it from the wall and lower it.

ALTERNATIVE FENCE SURFACES

Where screens are used as dividers in a garden, they are often very lightweight and intended more as a visual barrier to block a view. This gives you the opportunity to use lighter materials, such as bamboo strips **6**, thin hazel, willow strips, woven bamboo, brushwood or heather. The strength for these flimsy materials is provided by the posts and a support frame.

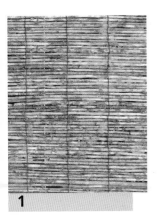

Alternatives to panel fences have become popular too. They can give your garden an entirely different look. This type of screening is lighter than wood and allows some light through, which should help your plants to grow while still giving them some shelter.

This type of screening fence does need to be fastened onto a stout framework (see page 94), but is easy to erect and can be changed every few years. It needs to be – it won't last as long as wooden panels.

A quick and simple way to transform an old or boring fence surface is to attach thin pieces of any of the above to the fence with either a hammer and nails **7**, or if it is a thin piece of screening you could use a heavy-duty stapler.

MAKING AND PUTTING UP SIMPLE SCREENING

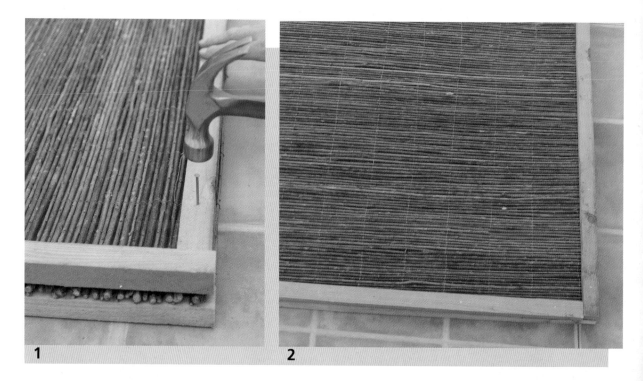

1

2

Lay out sections of the screening material, such as willow screen, on a flat open surface and cut it to size. Sections 1.8 x 1.8m (6 x 6ft) are about the largest you want to deal with. To make the frame, cut eight 1.8m (6ft) lengths of 50 x 25mm (2 x 1in) batten.

Place these battens around the margins of the screening material in pairs one under the material and one above. Drive 50mm (2in) galvanized nails through the top batten, through the screen and into the batten below so that it is trapped between two layers of batten **1**, and repeat this process all the way around the edge of the screen until you have a complete screen **2**.

Next mark out the site for the screen and identify positions for the support posts, for example at 1.8m (6ft) intervals, allowing extra for the batten overhang, then dig holes for the posts (see page 86). Fix the posts in place either with hardcore and concrete (see page 86) or metal spikes (see pages 90–91). Check with a spirit level to ensure that the post is upright.

Hold the screen up to the support posts and use galvanized nails or screws driven through the screen frame into the support posts at 300mm (12in) intervals up and down the posts **3**.

👍 **TOP TIP If you garden on a very windy site, you could consider erecting a fence of chicken wire or even chain link wire and attach the screening material to it later, fixing it into position with small galvanized wire twists.**

3

outdoor projects

The garden itself is finally finished, but apart from the plants it's a tad on the empty side! So here are a few simple projects anyone with a saw and hammer can attempt. You can save money and achieve great satisfaction when somebody is sitting on a nice bench, and you say 'I made that!'

tommy's bolt box

Not everyone has a garden, and anyone who lives in a flat or apartment may not have access to garden soil at all – but when did a small problem like that ever deter the really keen gardener? This is where container gardening can come into its own.

MAKING THE BOX

Wood is an obvious material to use because it is natural and easy to work with, but other materials can be added to it to provide an interesting, decorative finish. The completed container must be strong enough to withstand the weight and pressures of the compost inside, especially when the plants have just been watered – immediately after watering, the filled container can increase in weight four- or five-fold.

One method of increasing the strength of a container is to use lengths of threaded metal rod (or 'studding'), which can be cut to the required length and used to strengthen the whole structure of the planter.

Start by cutting the sides and ends of the planter to length from 12mm (½in) exterior-grade plywood – I made the box 915 x 300mm (3ft x 12in), but you can vary the dimensions to suit your requirements. On the sides make a mark 110mm (4½in) in from each bottom corner and draw a line connecting this point to the top corner. Cut

the sides along this line to create an angle **1**. Drill five 12mm (½in) bolt holes in each side, two in each end at the top and bottom and one in the centre, just above the base. Next, fix the two sides together with a G-cramp and drill holes through both sides at once **2** – this saves time and guarantees that both sets of holes are in identical positions. Fasten the sides and ends together with 15mm (⅝in) screws **3**.

Measure and cut the base to fit within the sides and ends, and then fasten the base in position with 19mm (¾in) screws through the sides and ends **4**. With a hacksaw, cut five lengths of 12mm (½in) threaded rod ('studding') 19mm (¾in) longer than the total width of the sides and ends **5**, and use a small metal file to smooth the cut ends of the rods **6**. Insert the rods through one side of the planter and push them through until the ends emerge through the opposite side **7**, then secure them with washers and nuts. Turn the planter

1   2   3

4

5

6

7

8

9

upside down, and drill a series of 12mm (½in) drainage holes in the base of the box **8**; cover inside the drainage holes with small squares of material cut from tights. So you can move the filled box without rupturing yourself, turn it upside down and fix four heavy-duty castors to the corners of the base with screws **9** – don't skimp and use castors that won't be up to the job.

To add more interest to the planter, some form of decoration can be added, such as sections of copper flashing cut into shapes and tacked onto the front and sides. Copper will look particularly attractive as it weathers and takes on a verdigris effect.

👍 **TOP TIP When drilling drainage holes in the base of the planter, allow one 25mm (1in) drainage hole for about every 300 x 300mm (12 x 12in) of surface at the top of the box.**

tommy's all-purpose box

Most of us would like a large garden so that we can install all the things we would like to have from our 'wish list'. This rarely happens, and items in the garden have to be multi-functional, with different uses at different times. This basic box can be adapted to a number of uses, which are shown on the following pages.

THE BASIC BOX

With a little planning, it is possible to make some of the things you intend to construct into something a little more multi-purpose and adaptable. That way, one basic item can be adapted for several purposes over a period of time. The finished size is up to you, and the size I have given you can easily be adapted. Always use pressure-treated softwood and exterior plywood for any outdoor project,

Cut four lengths of 915 x 150 x 50mm (36 x 6 x 2in) wood to form the side boards of the box, and cut a 45-degree angle at each end of the side board **1**, using a mitre box or saw. In each of the boards, drill three equidistant pilot holes in one end and two in the other. Join the four boards together with 50mm (2in) screws, staggering the screws so they do not meet **2**. Measure and cut a base from 19mm (¾in) exterior-grade plywood so that it fits the box frame.

Cut four blocks to make 100 x 100 x 50mm (4 x 4 x 2in) feet, and align them with the corners of the base,

resting on the 50mm (2in) ends. Drill pilot holes in the corners of the base and down through into the feet. Fasten the feet to the base with 50mm (2in) screws, driving the screws through the base into the feet **3**. Drill four 19mm (¾in) drainage holes in the base **4**, and tack screening over them (see page 97) **5**. Turn the frame over and fit the base onto the frame until it is flush with all of the sides, then screw the base in place with 75mm (3in) screws **6**.

This basic box can be adapted for use as a cold frame to shelter plants over winter (see page 102), or as a sandpit for a child's play area (see page 101); if it is lined with a waterproof material it could even become a water feature or raised pond (see page 100). Finally, it can also be lined with thinner plastic so it can be used as a small garden feature such as a herb garden (see opposite) or taken indoors and used for indoor plants – the possibilities are endless!

1   2   3   4

7

PAINTING THE BOX

Selecting a paint or wood preservative to protect the wood is particularly important, especially where the box may be used by or near children. Ideally, the box should be painted at least once a year, with particular attention paid to any joints and places where the wood has been cut across the grain **7**.

Stencils can be used to pick out figures and symbols over the painted surfaces of the sandpit to make it more interesting for children (see page 101).

GARDEN BOX

The basic box also makes an excellent raised bed in which to grow plants, but it should be lined with plastic or a pond liner to prevent the compost drying out too quickly, and to protect the wood.

In this instance, you should cut a series of about six 25–38mm (1–1½in) slits in the liner along the bottom edge of the sides to allow for water drainage. This box would make an ideal mini-herb garden **8**, situated outdoors close to the house, or an indoor plant box for your conservatory **9**.

8

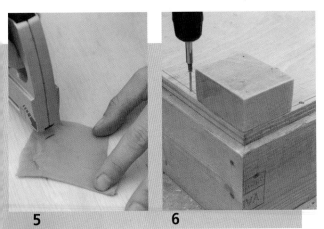

5

6

9

WATER FEATURE

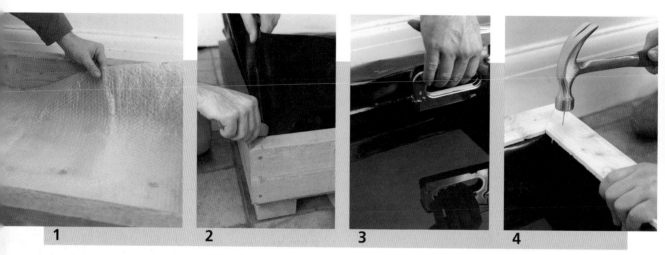

1 **2** **3** **4**

The basic box also makes an excellent water feature,
ideal for marginal plants that prefer to grow in shallow
water or just wet soil. It is worth lining the bottom of
the box with bubble plastic or old carpet, to protect the
liner from being punctured by splinters **1**. To make the
box waterproof, line it with heavy-duty polythene or a
sheet of pond-lining fabric, laid out in the bottom of the
box and folded up the sides **2**. Using black lining helps
to give the impression that the water inside the box is
much deeper than is actually the case.

You will find that the most difficult part is making
neat corners in the lining inside the box, but if you fold
the corners and half-fill the box with water so that the
pressure of the water holds the corner folds in place,
you can do this much more easily. Slit the corners with a
craft knife and fold the sides over the top.

The sides of the pond liner are held in place by
leaving a surplus of about 100mm (4in) of liner around
the top edge of the box; staple this to the top edge of
the box **3**. Cut four pieces of wood to cover the top
edges of the box, mitring the corners. Insert a water
pump and put the wire over one of the top edges, then
nail the wooden tops over the exposed liner with 38mm
(1½in) wire nails **4** – check the position before you take
up the hammer to avoid nailing through the wire!

CHILD'S SANDPIT

Young children love playing with sand, but unless it is kept under control, the sand has a tendency to end up everywhere except where it should be. A pit or container, especially if it can be covered, will keep the sand clean and in one place, and provide a reasonable depth of sand to play in. This type of play area is quite simple to construct, and with some thought beforehand, need occupy very little garden space. Follow the construction method described for the all-purpose box on pages 98–99, adapting the sizes as required. Remember to keep the lid on the box when not in use, or the sand will get too wet or, worse, the local cats will think you have constructed a loo just for them!

MAKING A LID

Make the basic box as described on page 96, but without the drainage holes. Measure the external width and length of the box, and cut a section of heavy-duty industrial grade plywood to fit the external dimensions of the sandpit. Cut this section of plywood in half, and sand all the cut surfaces to create rounded edges and remove any splinters. Cut a 50 x 19mm (2 x ¾in) strip of felt and glue and tack it to one edge of one section of the plywood, with 22mm (⅞in) over the edge of the lid.

Fasten two piano or strap hinges on the outer edge of one half of the lid and repeat this process on the other half of the lid. Place the two halves of the lid on the box, making sure that the centre edges of the lid are touching and covered by the felt overlap. Fasten the ends of the hinges onto the outer edges of the box. Paint the lid sections of the sandpit with wood preservative, varnish or paint, and leave them to dry.

VEGETABLE STORE

Through the winter months, when it is too cold and wet for children to play outdoors in a sandpit, both the sand and the box can be put to very good use. Providing the sand is clean and damp (but not wet), the box will make an excellent vegetable store, especially for root vegetables such as carrots, parsnips and potatoes, rather than leaving them in the cold wet soil.

Start by placing a 25–50mm (1–2in) layer of sand in the bottom of the box, and place a layer of vegetables over the surface of the sand, leaving about 19mm (¾in) between each one. Cover the vegetables with another 25–50mm (1–2in) layer of sand and repeat this process until the box is three-quarters full.

Make sure you keep the lid closed so the vegetables do not rot, and always wash the vegetables before they are stored, which will prevent the sand from being contaminated with garden soil.

TOMMY'S ADVICE

Placing a strip of roofing felt across the join in the lid will help to keep out the rain. The lid will keep the sand drier and deter the neighbourhood moggies.

COLD FRAME

To adapt the basic box for a cold frame, you need to add sloping sides and a lid. Cut three 450mm (18in) lengths of 75 x 50mm (3 x 2in) pressure-treated softwood to form the back and front boards of the box, two 150mm (6in) lengths of 75 x 50mm (3 x 2in) for the sides, and one 150 x 150 x 50mm (6 x 6 x 2in) length. Cut this last piece diagonally to make two slanting sections for the sides **1**. Drill pilot holes in the front, one back and one side board and screw them together to make a frame. Drill pilot holes in the sloping sides **2** and other back piece, and position them on top of the frame.

Cut two 150mm (6in) lengths of 50 x 50mm (2 x 2in) wood to form corner posts, position them at the back of the box with the bottom edges matching, then mark and cut the top so that it does not protrude beyond the top of the sloping sides or top back piece. Drill pilot holes through the corner posts into the two back pieces and four sides, and attach them with screws **3**, **4**.

Drill a pilot hole through the top of the angled board (about 150mm/6in from the front), then insert a 75mm (3in) screw to hold the sloping side in place **5**. Repeat this process on the opposite side of the box. Measure and cut a piece of heavy-duty exterior-grade plywood for the base of the frame and nail it into position, then cut and attach feet. Both these steps are shown in the instructions for the basic box on page 98.

1 2 3 4 5

6   **7**   **8**

MAKING THE LID

The back of the lid is a 450mm (18in) length of wood, and the sides are two 150mm (6in) lengths of 75 x 50mm (3 x 2in) wood. The front of the lid is 450 x 50 x 50mm (18 x 2 x 2in). Using a router, cut a 12mm (½in) wide groove 19mm (¾in) deep along the 50mm (2in) edge of all four pieces **6**. Position the three sections together to form three sides of a rectangle, with the grooved face matching on the inside. Clamp to hold in position and drill pilot holes, then screw the pieces together, making sure that the internal angles remain at right angles.

Cut a sheet of 10mm (⅜in) double-walled plastic or Perspex to fit the grooves in the lid of the frame and carefully slide it into place in the grooves **7**. Position the front piece with the groove fitting onto the plastic, then drill pilot holes and fasten the front to the side pieces.

Firmly support the lid about 3mm (⅛in) from the back of the frame, parallel to the top back edge, then mark the positions of screw holes for at least three hinges on both the bottom back edge of the lid and the top back edge of the frame. Drill the pilot holes and then screw the hinges in place **8**.

greenhouse growing bag holder

Temporary containers such as growing bags are great, but they do have limitations: they lack depth and are unable to support tall plants, even those with a short lifespan of one season or less. This lack of depth also makes it difficult to use canes or other supports to hold up plants. One way of overcoming this problem is to build a frame around the container and attach the supports to this.

HIDING YOUR GROWING BAG

Not all of the plants that are grown in containers have a long period of life – in fact, many plants have a short lifespan. For many edible plants such as vegetables, which grow rapidly and mature quickly, the appearance of the container is not particularly important, because it will soon be hidden by the crop's, foliage and as soon as they are gathered, it will be emptied.

A wide range of salad vegetables, fruit and flowers can be grown in polythene bags. Many of these plants will be quite happy in a container such as a growing bag, which is purely functional and nothing much to look at, but contains the plant nutrients to do the job. Although growing bags are seen by most gardeners as a once-only container, many can be used for a second season. Grow tomatoes in them the first season, and in the second year the same container of compost can be used to grow salad plants such as lettuce, radish and

salad onions. These will feed on the fertilizer residue from the tomato crop.

MAKING THE CONTAINER

Measure two lengths of 100 x 20mm (4 x ¾in) timber to exactly the same size as the length of the growing bag, then measure two lengths of timber to the same width. Mark the dimensions carefully on the timber and, using a square, draw lines with a pencil to indicate where the cuts are to be made **1**. Cut the timber to size to form both sides and the two ends for the frame **2**.

Drill both ends of each of the long sections of timber to form pilot holes for the screws; position the holes 25mm (1in) from the edges and 12mm (½in) from the end of each side board. Turn one of the short lengths of planking on its end and fix a long plank to it using screws **3**. Repeat with the other two sections of

1   2   3   4

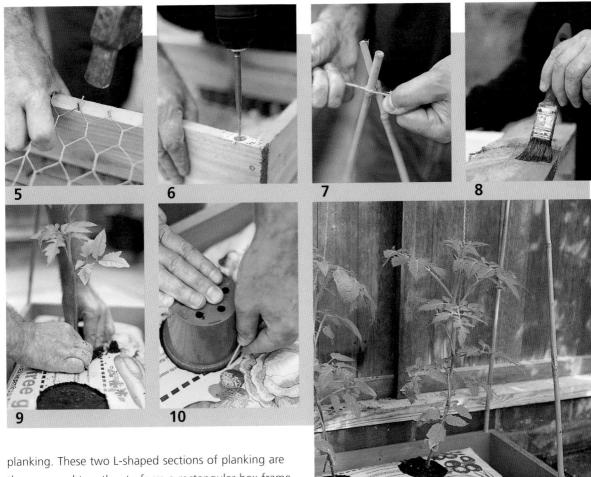

planking. These two L-shaped sections of planking are then screwed together to form a rectangular box frame. Lay the box frame flat and cut a section of 12mm (½in) chicken wire mesh to cover the base of the wooden frame. Stretch the wire taughtly over the box frame and staple the wire mesh to the edges of the timber **4**. Snap off the overhanging wire, and hammer down the cut ends **5** to avoid catching yourself all the time. Turn the frame over and drill two 19mm (¾in) holes (about 75mm/3in deep) **6**, at both ends of each of the long boards, a short distance in from the sides.

Place the growing bag in the frame and insert four stout canes in the drilled holes at each end of the frame. Pull the two canes together so that they cross over at the top and tie them together with string **7**. Take out the canes and paint the box **8**. Put back the canes and tie another cane horizontally from one set of crossed canes to the other (about 50mm/2in below the top of

the upright canes). Position the plants in the growing bag **9**, and water them well to eliminate any air pockets and to allow the compost to settle.

👍 **TOP TIP Use an upturned plastic flowerpot as a template for cutting the holes. This gives you a clean-cut hole 10.**

Tie long strings to the horizontal cane and lower them to the base of each plant. Tie the strings around the base of each plant. As the plants grow, they can be twisted around the string, which will provide support **11**.

making an H-base bench

If you have a half-decent garden, the best thing to do is enjoy it. And to do that, all you need is a simple bench to sit on, relax and watch the plants grow. You can even consider making the bench a little bit longer so that you can lounge on it rather than just sitting down.

A SIMPLE WOODEN BENCH

These days there is a tendency to have very elaborate furniture, which is not surprising with the garden being treated as an outdoor room by many people. Simple, well-made garden furniture, especially when wood is used, will usually fit into just about any garden situation and not look out of place.

Start by cutting the sections of wood to the correct length:
• two 50 x 200mm (2 x 8in) top boards for the seat, cut to a length of 1.5m (5ft),
• four pieces of 50 x 75mm (2 x 3in) cut to 400mm (16in) long to form the legs of the bench,
• two pieces of 50 x 75mm (2 x 3in) cut to 250mm (10in) long to form the leg braces,
• two pieces of 50 x 75mm (2 x 3in) cut to 310mm (12½in) long for support rails.

On the ends of the two leg braces, with a carpenter's square, mark out half-joints 20mm (1in) deep and 40mm (1½in) along the brace **1**. Cut a 20mm (1in) deep saw cut across the brace at the 40mm (1½in) marks **2**. Place the brace sections in a vice or work-bench clamp and, using a broad-bladed wood chisel and a hammer, cut out a 20mm (1in) deep and 40mm (1½in) long section from the ends of each brace **3**.

Drill two pilot holes through each section of half-joint. Start the assembly by positioning the leg brace half way up the bench legs to make sure they will fit **4**. Apply a layer of waterproof glue over the ends of the braces, and fit the legs and braces together using 80mm (3½in) long screws. Screw from the outside of the braces, through into the leg to close up the joints and make them glue together more securely **5**. Next, place the

support rails against the top of the leg assembly, so that the top of the support rail is flush with the top of the leg assembly, **6**. Apply a layer of waterproof glue over the areas where the sections of wood are to be joined, and fit the legs and support rails together using 80mm (3½in) long screws.

Once the leg assembly is complete, smooth down the wood with sandpaper to remove any rough edges or splinters **7**. Place the seat boards face down on a flat,

level surface and mark the positions of each leg assembly on the seat boards, about 200mm (8in) in from each end of the boards **8**. Apply a layer of glue over the top surface of the support rails (the surface that will come into contact with the seating boards), and position a leg assembly on the seating boards (glued surface downwards). Using 100mm (4in) long screws fasten the support rail to the underside of the seating boards **9**. The screws are positioned diagonally from the support

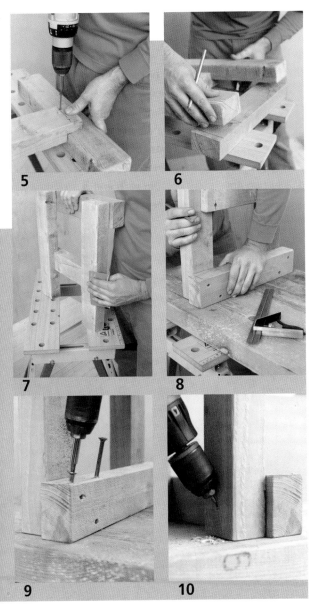

rail to the legs so that the seat board can be fixed at an angle. Repeat this process on the second leg assembly at the other end of the seat.

👍 TOP TIP **Screwing through the support rails from the underside of the bench into the seating boards prevents water settling into any of the screw holes and getting into the joints.**

To provide extra strength in the joints, a 100mm (4in) long screw can be driven at an angle through the top of each bench leg into the top board **10**. The completed bench can now be righted and placed in position, but allow a couple of hours for the glue to dry before using it.

A wood preservative paint can be applied to the surfaces of the bench, but make sure the underside of the bench is also treated so that all of the wood surfaces react to the weather in the same way. The preservative should be applied once a year to keep the wood protected; this also gives you the opportunity to change the colour scheme if you decide to move the seat to a new position.

👍 TOP TIP **When you paint or re-paint the seat always pay particular attention to the bottom of each leg, where the wood has been cut across the grain and is in contact with the ground – this means it is the most likely place to rot, so give it a double coat.**

making an obelisk

Ornamental structures such as obelisks are very good for supporting plants, but they should not be so heavy or intrusive that they dominate the garden and dwarf the plants they are supporting. It is also better not to use heavy grade timber or the plants will not be able to twine around the obelisk and may need tying in to make full use of the support.

HOW TO MAKE AN OBELISK

These narrow, pyramid-like frames are used as free-standing, upright structures, which not only support plants but can be interesting as focal points in the garden. If your obelisk is intended to be a feature in its own right, it must be noticeable, and this can be achieved either by using an unusual material from which to make the obelisk or using various paints.

Where the obelisk is used mainly as a plant support, the side panels should be filled in in some way so that the plants are provided with something to lean against or grip hold of.

CUTTING THE WOOD
Start by cutting four sections of 50 x 50mm (2 x 2in) timber to a length of 1.65m (5½ft). Now cut four pieces of 50 x 25mm (2 x 1in) wood 590mm (23½in) long to form the tie bars for the bottom of the obelisk. Then cut four pieces of the same size wood 110mm (4½in) long for the top. Clamp all these pieces of wood together **1**. Take the long 'legs' and, using a carpenter's square, draw a pencil line 100mm (4in) up from the bottom across all four legs **2**. Separate these legs and draw the pencil line around all four sides of each leg.

Prepare the tie bars for fixing to the uprights by drilling two 4mm (³⁄₁₆in) holes in each end **3**. Countersink the holes so that the screw heads lie flush with the surface of the wood.

ASSEMBLING THE OBELISK
Assemble the first side of the obelisk by laying two legs out on a flat surface in a triangular shape, and align the lower side of the long tie bar with the pencilled lines

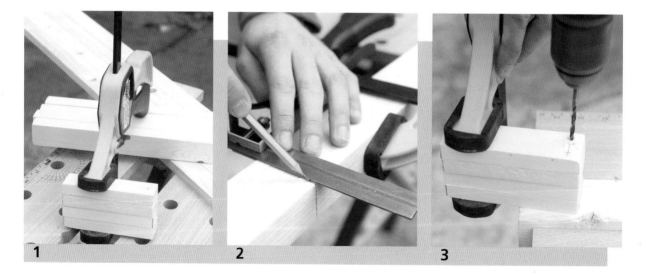

1   2   3

made earlier on the bottoms of the legs **4**. Put one screw through the bottom tie bar into each leg, and a single screw through the top tie bar into each leg. Once you are satisfied that everything is positioned correctly, continue to screw on the top and bottom tie bars. Repeat this process with the second triangle. You can speed things up a bit by using the first triangle as a template.

Working on a flat surface, tilt the two triangles on their edge and screw on a bottom tie bar **5** and a top tie bar **6**. It helps to have two people for this. Turn the framework over and repeat this process with the remaining side to complete the framework of the obelisk.

Now measure sections of 15 x 25mm (⅝ x 1in) batten for the intermediate tie bars. Mark **7**, and cut them before drilling a 2mm (⅒in) pilot hole in each end to avoid splitting the wood. Fasten the battens to the obelisk legs using 25mm (1in) screws **8**. At least four battens should be used on each side, but you may prefer to use more to provide extra rigidity.

Fill in the screw holes with filler and paint the structure with a suitable garden paint or preservative.

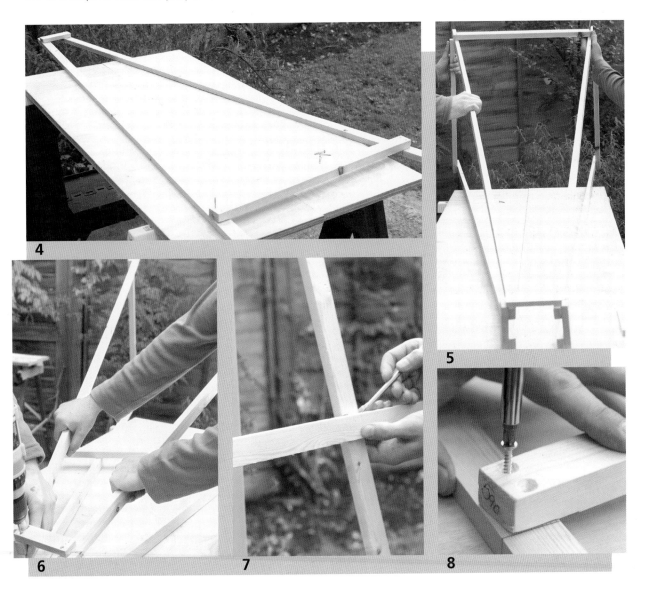

4

5

6

7

8

1
2
3

4
5
6

CAPPING THE OBELISK

To finish the obelisk, cut a piece of 25mm (1in) thick timber 135mm (5½in) square and drill a 20mm (¾in) hole through the centre. This will form the capping piece, which can be screwed on to the tops of the four legs using two 40mm (1½in) screws. Chamfer the edges **1** so that the water can run off it. Then select a 220mm (8½in) long offcut of 50 x 50mm (2 x 2in) wood. Mark the centre by drawing two diagonal lines **2** and drilling where they meet. Drill a 20mm (¾in) hole to a depth of 50mm (2in) into the middle of the base **3**. Now draw a pencil line around it 150mm (6in) from the top, and mark a line across the centre at the top **4**. Using a saw, cut from the top line down to the line on two sides to create a wedge **5**, and cut again from the top down to the lower line on the two remaining sides to form a spike. Then cut a 75mm (3in) length of 20mm (¾in) dowel, apply wood glue to one end and insert it into the capping piece. Apply glue to the protruding end and push the spike down on the dowel until it is seated on the capping piece. Paint the spike and capping piece and, finally, screw the capping piece onto the top of the obelisk **6**.

👍 **TOP TIP It is much easier to drill the base of the spike before it has been cut to shape rather than afterwards.**

making a dustbin hide

It is quite common to use a screen to disguise or hide unsightly objects in the garden, but as a project it is rarely tackled. Done properly, you can provide screening without blocking out valuable light. So, what have you got to hide?

HOW TO MAKE A SCREEN

The most obvious candidate for a disguise in your garden is the dustbin (which may be close to the house entrance) where your refuse is stored until it is collected. The trick is to hide the bin but in such a way as to make sure that it is still easily accessible when you take out the rubbish, and does not hinder the refuse collection team. A simple screen will do the trick, because the aim is to mask the bin from view rather than make it secure. Often, a box made from a close-meshed trellis will do the job, or you can use fencing trellis, but this will need some cladding such as hessian or fleece, due to the large size of the mesh – often 100–150mm (4–6in).

Start by measuring the objects you want to hide. If you have more than one rubbish bin for your household, you will need to increase the dimensions to accommodate them. Here, we want to hide two dustbins, but you could adapt this project to hide a wheelie bin by increasing the size of the panels. The screening we have used for this particular hide is shown on page 94. You will need to make four pieces of panel, each large enough to hide the dustbins properly.

Cut four posts from 75 x 75mm (3 x 3in) wood – their length depends on your panel size. This hide is moveable, its sheer weight and size keep it secure, so we have not sunk the posts. If you intend to sink the posts into the ground (see page 23), increase their length by 25 per cent. Attach each of the two side panels to two of the posts, one at each end. Screw straight through the panel into the posts, which will be on the inside of the hide **1**.

The two smaller end panels are attached flush with the side panels that are already secured to the posts – so both the posts and side panels lie inside the end panels.

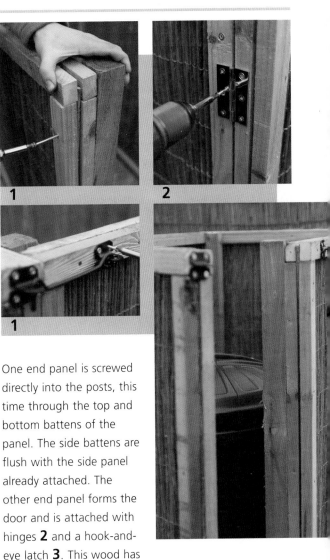

1

2

1

One end panel is screwed directly into the posts, this time through the top and bottom battens of the panel. The side battens are flush with the side panel already attached. The other end panel forms the door and is attached with hinges **2** and a hook-and-eye latch **3**. This wood has been treated, but you can paint the panel with a garden paint or wood preservative to disguise it further.

👍 **TOP TIP If you wish, you can make a fifth panel to act as a lid, which can be hinged to make it easier to open so as to reach the top of the bin.**

electricity in your garden

It's quite common to plug garden tools into the nearest indoor socket and run a cable out through the nearest window or door. This often results in long extension leads trailing around, which can prove extremely hazardous and turn your garden into quite an obstacle course. Alternatively fit an outdoor socket.

INSTALLING AN OUTSIDE ELECTRICAL SUPPLY

Electrical sockets can be mounted outside provided they are well protected against the weather – water and electricity do NOT mix. If you install a weatherproof mains socket outdoors, mount it high enough to prevent it being struck by tools and machinery or hidden by plants. All work MUST be inspected by a qualified electrician.

A simple way to put in an outside supply is to take it directly off an existing socket. This is viable if you have a socket close to an outside wall, but if it is too far away the method shown here is an better alternative. Start indoors by locating the cable of the ring main you wish to

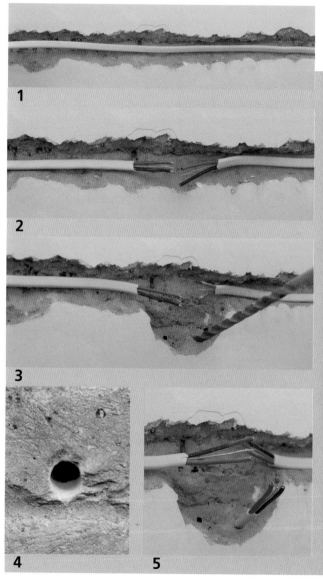

1

2

3

4   5

TOMMY'S ADVICE

According to the Wiring Regulations, any socket supplying mains power to garden tools or equipment must be fitted with a residual current device (RCD) with a trip rating of 30 milliamps. This device will switch off automatically as soon as a fault is detected, before anyone using the equipment can receive an electric shock. You can provide RCD protection in several ways: have a unit with its own built-in residual current device (see above); fit a separate RCD near the consumer unit so that it protects the whole ring circuit, including a spur for garden equipment; or use an adaptor incorporating an RCD. RCDs fitted in adapters or plugs provide some protection, but do not satisfy the Regulations for the socket itself to be protected.

use as your electricity supply. Switch off at the mains or remove the fuse for the circuit at the mains supply board before carefully exposing the cable **1**. This involves removing plaster from the wall and cutting through the cable of the ring main. Expose the wires in the cable and bend the ends of the cable out of the way **2** before marking the dimensions of a junction box at the point where the cable was originally joined. Using a masonry chisel, chop out a recess in the wall to hold the junction box. At the back of the recess for the junction box, drill a hole through the wall with a masonry drill **3** (this may be up to 300mm (12in) long if you are drilling a cavity wall). Drill at a slight angle so that the hole on the outer side of the wall is slightly lower than on the inside to keep water

out **4**. Thread cable through the wall **5** and push it through the back of the junction box, before fastening the junction box into the recess with two screws (the rim must be flush with the wall's surface). Connect the ends of the three cables inside the junction box **6**, by stripping off the plastic insulation with wire strippers to expose a length of wire at each end. Match up the same coloured wires from each of the three cable sections and screw them together in the terminals of the junction box as shown; place the cover on the box. On the outside wall, connect the cable into an outdoor switched socket **7**. Before replacing the cover of the socket, turn it over and fit it onto the wall. Fill the hole around the cable with a waterproof sealant. The socket is now ready for testing **8**.

before starting any electrical work, make sure that the circuit you are working on is switched off

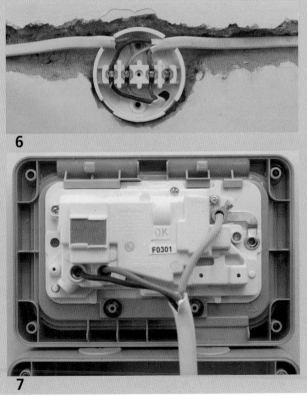

6

7

8

lighting your garden

Outdoor lighting is popular either for illuminating the garden or, more commonly, for safety and security. It enables us to see where we are walking and satisfies our curiosity about who is out there. We can even have a camera mounted to view the garden via the TV screen, to see what is going on without getting out of our chairs.

CHOOSING YOUR LIGHTING

You have installed your outside point for any electrical work you need to do in the garden, so now is the time to think about lighting your garden. We spend a lot of time designing the garden, putting down patios or decking, fences or walls, but we often forget about the garden after dark. With long summer nights you really should consider installing lighting in your garden. There are many lights now that can be totally unobtrusive in the day **1** and bring out the best in your plants at dusk **2**.

There are lights that simply attach to your parasol **3**, for illuminating your eating, or lighting up your decking **4**. There are lights that can help you to find your way on paths or just show you the way **5**. You can put in lights that disguise themselves as rocks **6** or lights that illuminate dramatically your best architectural plants **7**. Do have soft lights that show up some of your prettiest planting. And don't forget your pond; a normal daytime water feature **8** becomes fabulous at nightime **9**.

1

2

3

5

4

6

7

8

9

INSTALLING GARDEN LIGHTING

WALL-MOUNTED LIGHTING

This is ideal for improving visibility, particularly near paths and steps, as perception of depth and distance is hampered if the light level drops. These lights take up very little room and the range of shapes and fittings available means they can look attractive. Alternatively, they can remain unnoticed until they are actually in use.

Lights with a passive infra-red (PIR) sensor, which will usually switch the light on within seconds of detecting movement across the sensor beam, are ideal for both visibility and security. These can be linked to a video camera mounted on the wall and then linked to your television as a closed circuit surveillance system.

INSTALLING SECURITY LIGHTING

After fitting the electric connection for running electricity to the outside, decide where the light is to be sited and mark the position. Measure out the correct length of cable and fix it to the wall using cable clips **1**.

If you are fitting it to a brick wall, where possible, fix the cable along the lines of a mortar joint to help disguise its presence. Mark the wall **2** to indicate where the wall mountings for the light are to be fitted and drill the wall at the marked positions. Fit wall plugs into the drill holes. Screw the back plate to the wall and, following the instructions, connect the cable to the terminals in the light fitting **3** before inserting the light bulb and fitting on the glass bowl. The finished light is now ready for use after connecting up to the circuit inside **4**.

👍 **TOP TIP Always try to mount security lights and cameras out of reach so that they cannot be disabled by intruders. Mount them at least 2.4m (8ft) above the ground.**

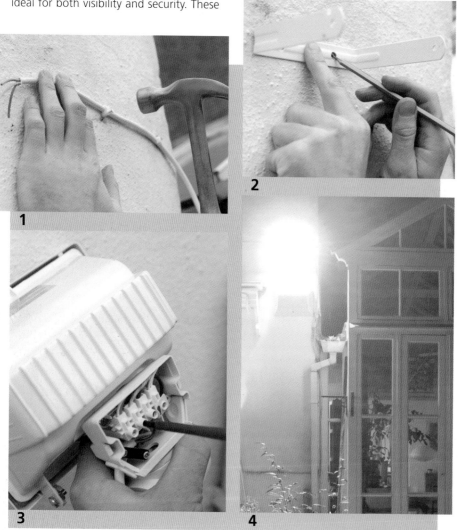

1

2

3

4

electricity is used, you need armour-coated cable or a cable that will shut down if it is damaged in any way. These systems are best laid by a specialist contractor.

With safety in mind, if fitting a lighting system yourself, it is best to opt for one of the many low-voltage (12-volt) systems available. These usually connect to mains electricity via a transformer positioned either on a wall outside in a weatherproof box, or indoors close to the power supply. Follow the manufacturer's instructions exactly when you connect up the low-voltage cable to the transformer.

Lay out the cables and press the bayonet connections together, making sure the cables are positioned correctly in the clips and the clips are pressed firmly into position.

Connect the end of each run of cable into the transformer housing **1**. Press it firmly into place to ensure that a good connection is established before simply plugging the transformer into the mains supply **2**.

Lay out the cables and switch on the system to check that all lights are working before you bury cables in the border **3**. Try to bury the main cable along the edge of a path so it is easy to find should you need to.

Finally, wait until dusk, as the daylight starts to dip, before switching on the system and positioning the lights. Adjust them to light up the plants or areas you wish to illuminate – it may take minor adjustments over several evenings until you are happy with the effect.

INSTALLING LOW-VOLTAGE LIGHTING

There are many electric lighting systems of either high- or low-voltage rating that you can use. In the end, the type and size of lighting system you want in your garden comes down to personal preference (see page 58).

Mains electricity, with a 240-volt rating, will power garden lighting and do an excellent job. But there is always a potential risk of injury should the live cable be damaged while you work in the garden. Where mains

TOMMY'S ADVICE

Where possible, disguise or camouflage the light fitting in or around low-growing plants – it's the light you want to see, not the fittings. This has the added advantage of giving some drama at dusk to your garden, but in the day it is just an ordinary plant.

fitting an outside tap

Watering can be the most tedious task in the garden, especially in the height of summer when the job can seem never-ending. Half an hour after you have finished, the plants look just as dry again and the more you give them the more they want.

PLUMBING IN A TAP

If there is one thing all plants have in common, it is the need for water to make them grow, and in the summer they need lots of it. The easiest way to water your plants is with a hosepipe. Having an outside tap stops all the mess and bother of having to open windows or doors and drag in a hosepipe to connect to an indoor tap.

A tap fitted to an outside wall is very convenient for attaching a hosepipe – for washing the car, watering your garden, or fitting an irrigation system.

TAPPING INTO THE MAINS

By using compression joints, it is possible to add a section of pipe to the indoor water supply and have water outdoors. Usually, it is the pipe leading to the cold tap beneath the kitchen sink that works best. Most domestic cold water pipes will be 15mm (⅝in), so a small section of 15mm (⅝in) pipe can be added for an outside tap.

Start by turning off the stopcock and draining as much water out of the pipe as possible by turning the cold tap on and leaving it to run dry – no matter how hard you try, some water will remain in the pipe.

Mark a point on the cold water pipe and cut out a 3mm (⅛in) section with a hacksaw **1**. At the point where the small section of pipe has been removed, drill a hole from the inside out through the wall using a masonry drill. This hole should be large enough to accommodate the diameter of the pipe **2**. Measure a length of pipe that is long enough to run through the wall. Fasten a bib tap to one end of this pipe **3**, screwing it tightly into place.

Inside, fit a compression T-piece over the cut ends of the cold water pipe with the centre hole in the T-piece joint pointing into the hole drilled through the wall **4**. The T-piece is easy to fit, all you need is two adjustable spanners to tighten the T-piece onto the pipe.

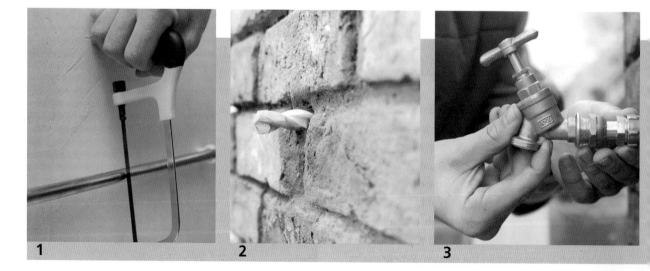

1   2   3

5

Push the opposite end of the pipe, which is connected to the bib tap, through the wall (from the outside), and push it into the centre hole in the T-piece joint.

I suggest that at this stage you fit a gate valve somewhere on the run so you can turn off the supply during cold weather **5**. Every winter, when you turn off the supply, you must turn the inside tap to 'off' and the outside tap to 'on', and drain off any residue.

👍 **TOP TIP A check valve must be fitted to any water supply going outdoors to prevent contaminated water being drawn back into the mains water system. Fit the check valve into the plumbing or as a connection between the hosepipe and the tap.**

FIXING AN EASY-TO-FIT TAP

If you can't be bothered to do proper plumbing for the tap, buy a kit. Kits come with all the fittings ready supplied, including push-fit fittings, a length of hose, the tap and a self-cutting plumbing-in-valve **6**. The self-

4

cutting valve will pierce and seal the existing pipe without you having to do any major plumbing! The only disadvantage is that the hose attachment will be seen outside and the connections are not as secure as a plumbed-in tap.

Drill a hole from the inside out through the wall using a masonry drill. As before, this

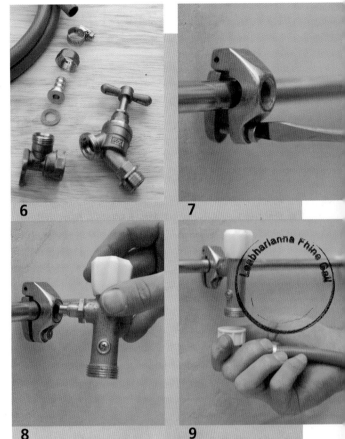

6 **7**

8 **9**

hole should be large enough for the diameter of the hose. Screw the saddle over the exposed pipe into the wall **7**. This will provide a firm fixing for the valve. Now screw in the valve **8**, having made sure beforehand that it is in the 'off' position. Keep screwing in until you are sure that you have pierced the pipe. When you have finished, the valve must be in the down position.

Use an adjustable spanner to tighten up the lock nut on the valve on the saddle to ensure that the joint is waterproof. Screw on the hose to the valve outlet **9**. This threads through to the external wall to connect to the bib tap outside.

👍 **TOP TIP Try to keep any external pipe supply run to the bib tap as short as possible, since this is always vulnerable to freezing. I always cut and fit some foam pipe-insulation to the external supply pipe to reduce the likelihood of the pipe freezing.**

simple garden irrigation

If you don't have much spare time (or hate watering your garden), you could fit a low-pressure watering system to water the borders and save yourself one more tedious, labour-intensive job. Even better, you could fit a timer so that the garden is watered while you are asleep – and even when you're away on holiday.

GARDEN IRRIGATION

For watering your entire garden, a seeping hose system is ideal. It needs only standard hosepipe fittings and can be laid out anywhere. The water spreads out after it has soaked into the ground, reducing the amount lost by evaporation.

FITTING A WHOLE GARDEN SYSTEM
Lay out the piping to get the maximum amount of water to each plant (for established shrubs, position the pipe within 150–300mm/6–12in of the plant's base). Use the plastic pegs supplied to hold the pipe in the desired position **1** and connect it up to a water supply such as a hosepipe with hose connectors. Turn on the tap to allow the water to flow through the pipes, and check carefully to detect any large unintended leaks **2**. To give extra water to a particular plant, you can connect spurs off your system using a T piece union **3**. Simply cut the pipe and push it on to each end of the connector **4**.

1

2

3

4

5

6

7

to buy a kit which has all the components for all sizes of pots and hanging baskets, as well as the tap connectors.

Narrow-gauge black plastic tubes can be used for this. Just lay out the tube between the pots **5**. At each pot, cut through the tube and join up the ends to a small T-piece union.

👍 **TOP TIP Pushing the pipe on can be difficult, but if you simply warm the pipe in some hot water to expand it, voilá, it slips on easily 6.**

After this has been done, cut more lengths of tube (long enough to reach into each pot), place a tiny drip nozzle in one end of each tube and fasten the other end of the tube onto the 'leg' of the T-piece. Lay the end of the tube with the dripper nozzle in the pot, connect the main tube to the tap and start watering **7**.

For larger containers, place two or three nozzles in the pot – this will ensure that even the biggest plants get enough water **8**.

To make the system fully automatic, a battery-powered timing device can be fitted to the water supply **9**. This will make it possible for the watering system to work even when the gardener is on holiday.

8   9

FITTING A CONTAINER SYSTEM

For watering plants in containers on a patio or deck you need a system that delivers water directly into each container, rather than soaking the floor. The best thing is

glossary

Aggregate Crushed stone that is mixed with sand to make ballast and used to make concrete.

Angle iron A metal bar, usually made of steel or iron, L-shaped in cross section.

Ballast A combination of aggregate and sand used in concreting.

Balustrade A railing around a deck, made from timber or metal.

Base coat A flat coat of paint over which a layer of gloss is applied.

Bat A cut piece of brick, usually more than half a brick in length.

Batten A narrow strip of wood, usually used as a support or to make formwork.

Bevel Any angle at which two pieces of wood meet, other than a right angle.

Blind To cover hardcore with sand as a base for laying paving.

Bond Strength of adhesion; also the design in which bricks or blocks are laid – a stretcher bond has each course staggered by half a brick length over the previous one.

Bricklaying mortar Standard mortar for bricklaying is a mix of six parts sand, one part Portland cement and one part hydrated lime. Sometimes a plasticizer is used instead of lime to make it easier to work.

Builders' sand Also called soft sand, this is sand that has been washed to remove any impurities and salt.

Cavity wall A wall made of two separate, parallel masonry skins with an air space between them.

CCA Copper, cadmium and arsenic, the chemicals used to pressure-treat timber.

Cement In concrete and bricklaying mortars, Portland cement is generally used.

Cement mortar A grey or off-white mortar used for laying tiles, made up of three parts sand and one part Portland cement.

Chamfer A flat, narrow surface along the edge of a workpiece, usually (but not always) set at a 45 degree angle to any adjacent surfaces.

Concrete A mix of aggregate, cement and sand; the proportions vary depending on the use for the concrete.

Counterbore A tapered recess that allows the head of a screw or bolt to lie below a surface; also to cut such a recess.

Countersink To cut a tapered recess that allows the head of a screw or bolt to lie flush with a surface.

Course One level of bricks or blocks in masonry.

Cup To bend as a result of shrinkage; usually referred to as being across the length of a piece of wood.

Cure To finish a concrete surface so that it does not dry too rapidly and crack.

Damp-proof course (DPC) A layer of impervious material that prevents moisture rising through a wall.

Damp-proof membrane (DPM) A layer of impervious material that prevents moisture rising through a concrete slab or into a floor; usually polythene.

Datum line A line from which all other measurements are taken.

Decking The walking surface of a timber deck.

Earth A connection between the earth or ground and an electrical circuit; also a terminal to which this connection is made.

Face edge A woodworking term for a surface that is planed square to the face side (see below).

Face side A woodworking term for a flat, planed surface from which other angles and dimensions are measured and worked.

Fall A slope built into paving to make sure surface water is drained well.

Feather To smooth or work an edge until it is imperceptible.

Finial A decorative wooden or metal cap for a post.

Formwork A wooden frame with boards supported by stakes or pegs in the ground, used as a mould for the surface area and top level of a concrete slab.

Frog A recess pressed into a brick.

Going The width of a tread of the step.

Grain The direction of wood fibres in a particular workpiece; also a pattern on the surface of timber made by cutting through the fibres.

Hardcore Building rubble used as a base for concrete or paving.

Housing long, narrow channel cut across the general direction of wood grain to form part of a joint.

Joist A horizontal wooden or metal beam (such as an RSJ) used to support a structure such as a floor, ceiling or wall.

Key To roughen a surface to provide a better grip when it is being glued; also the surface so roughened.

Lime Hydrated lime is mixed with mortar to make it easier to work.

MDF Medium-density fibreboard, a man-made sheet material that can be worked like wood and is used as a substitute for it.

Mitre A joint between two pieces of wood formed by cutting 45 degree bevels at the end of each piece; also to cut such a joint.

Mitre saw A hand or power saw that can be set to cut mitres and bevels in wood.

PAR The acronym of planed all round, meaning timber that is planed smooth on all its faces.

Pergola A frame between a house and garden, used for shade and as a support for climbing plants; may be roofed, and can be freestanding, used as a walkway or attached to the house.

Pilot hole A small-diameter hole drilled to act as a guide for a screw thread.

Plasticizer A modern alternative to lime, used in mortar mixes.

Portland cement A grey or grey-blue cement used in most building work.

Post socket A square metal socket, bolted to concrete, into which the base of a post is fitted.

Pressure-treated timber Used for outdoor structures, this is timber that has had preservative applied under pressure; the chemicals used (copper, cadmium and arsenic) give the timber a green tinge.

Profile The outline or contour of an object.

RCD Residual circuit device, a device that monitors the flow of electrical current through the live and neutral wires of a circuit.

Rebate A stepped rectangular recess along the edge of a workpiece, usually forming part of a joint; also to cut such a recess.

Reinforcement bar A steel bar used with steel mesh to strengthen concrete.

Reveal The vertical side of an opening.

Riser The vertical part of a step.

Score To scratch a line with a pointed tool.

Screed A smooth layer of sand or mortar used as a base for paving; also to smooth the layer level.

Scribe To copy the profile of a surface on the edge of sheet material to be butted against it; also to mark a line with a pointed tool.

Sharp sand A coarse sand mixed with aggregate for making concrete and floor screeds.

Slurry A wet mixture of cement or clay and water, used in paving.

Sub-base A layer of gravel, hardcore rubble or crushed rock tamped to make a bed for sand in paving.

Tamp To compact a base or bedding layer by applying repeated pressure.

Template A cut-out pattern, made from paper, wood, metal etc., used to help shape a workpiece accurately.

Tongue-and-groove A timber joint in which the tongue along the edge of one board is fitted into a matching groove cut into the edge of another board.

Tread The horizontal part of a step.

Undercoat A layer or layers of paint used to cover primer and build up a protective layer before a top coat is applied.

index

suppliers

GARDEN SUPPLIERS

B&Q
Major DIY store for everything you need
tel: 0845 222 1000 for stockists
web: www.diy.com

ADRIAN HALL
Garden related goods, trade and retail
in South West London
tel: 0208 890 1778
web: www.adrianhall.co.uk

HILLHOUT
Garden products available worldwide,
tel: 01502 718091 – all calls
email: w.durrant@btconnect.com
web: www.hillout.com

LUXFORM LIGHTING
Garden lighting products available from
major garden centres
tel: 01564 775 532 for customer services
email: info@sourceboxltd.com
UK stockists: www.luxform.co.uk
full product range:www.luxform-lighting.com

MARSHALLS
A long established manufacturer of
flagstones and landscaping materials. The
Marshalls Register is an established
network of contractors. For details, call
the customer helpline or visit the website
tel: 0870 120 7474 for general enquiries
web: www.marshalls.co.uk

ROLAWN
Turf and lawn related products
tel: 01904 608 661
email: info@rolawn.co.uk
web: www.rolawn.co.uk

WESTMINSTER STONE
Merchants in natural stone and aggregates.
And a long established manufacturer of
flagstones and landscaping materials.
tel: 01978 710658
fax: 01978 710844
email: penny@westminsterstone.com
web: www.westminsterstone.com

WOODBLOCX
Wooden block-building system for the
garden
web: www.woodblocx.co.uk
tel: 0800 3891420 freephone helpline

PAINT SUPPLIERS

CROWN
tel: 0870 240 1127 paint talk helpline
web: www.crownpaint.co.uk

SADOLIN
tel: 01480 496 868 for woodcare advice
centre
email: woodcare@sis.akzonobel.com
web: www.sadolin.co.uk

SANDTEX
tel: 0870 240 1127 for paint talk helpline
web: www.sandtex.co.uk

TOOLS ETC

ATLAS COPCO
Milwaukee is a brand name within the
Atlas Copco Group
tel: 01442 222378 for nearest dealer
email: milwaukee@uk.atlascopco.com
web: www.milwaukee_et.com

BLACK & DECKER
Register online to receive latest product
information and DIY tips
tel: 01753 511234 for customer helpline
email: info@blackanddecker.co.uk
web: www.blackanddecker.co.uk

DE WALT
tel: 0700 433 9258 for stockists
email: via website
web: www.dewalt.co.uk

MARSHALLTOWN AND ESTWING TOOLS
(supplied by Rollins Group)
email: sales@rollins.co.uk
web: www.rollins.co.uk

SCREWFIX DIRECT
Order online, next day delivery, trade
prices
tel: 0500 414141
email: online@screwfix.com
web: www.screwfix.com

WACKER GB LIMITED
Compaction Plates – single direction and
reversible, block Splitters, submersible
Pumps, rammers and rollers
tel: 01488 681428
web: www.wackergroup.com

WOOD/OTHER MATERIALS

JEWSON
Products available worldwide
tel: 0800 539766 for customer services
email: customer.services@jewson.co.uk
web: www.jewson.co.uk

MAGNET
tel: 0845 123 6789 enquiries help line
email: via website
web: www.magnet.co.uk

photography credits

2–5 All David Murphy; **7–12** All Mike Newton; **13** David Murphy; **14-18** All Mark Winwood; **19** All Sarah Cuttle, (top right) Mark Winwood; **20-21** All Mark Winwood; **22** All David Murphy; **23-24** All Sarah Cuttle; **25-27** Mark Winwood; **28** (1-3) Mark Winwood, (4-6) Sarah Cuttle; **29-31** All Mark Winwood; **34-36** All Mark Winwood; **37-39** David Murphy; **40-41** (1) David Murphy, (2-4) AW's Amanda Heywood; **42-43** (1) David Murphy, (2) Westminster Stone; **44** Mike Newton; **45** All Mark Winwood; **46-47** (1) Mike Newton, (2-3) Mark Winwood, (4) Sarah Cuttle, (5-7) Mark Winwood, (8) Westminster Stone, (9) Mark Winwood; **48-49** (1) Mike Newton, (2) Mark Winwood, (3-4) Westminster Stone, (5-6) Mark Winwood ; **50-51** (1-3) Mark Winwood, (4-6) Hillhout; **52-53** (1) Hillhout, (2-4) Mark Winwood; **54-55** (1) Mike Newton, (2-3) Mark Winwood, (4) Hillhout, (5) Sarah Cuttle; **56-57** (1-3) Hillhout, (4) Sarah Cuttle; **58-59** (1) Marshalls, (2-4) Luxform, (5) Hillhout, (6) Luxform, (7-8) Sarah Cuttle; **60** (1) Marshalls, (2) Sarah Cuttle; **61** David Murphy; **62** All Mark Winwood; **63** All Mark Winwood (top) David Murphy; **64-65** All Mark Winwood; **66-67** (1) Mark Winwood, (2-3) Sarah Cuttle, (4) David Murphy, (5) Mike Newton, (6) Mark Winwood; **68-69** All Mark Winwood; **70-71** All Mark Winwood (far right) Sarah Cuttle; **72-73** All Mark Winwood (Tommy) David Murphy; **74** (1-4) Sarah Cuttle, (bottom left) Westminster Stone; **75** All Sarah Cuttle; **76-77** (1-3) Mark Winwood, (4-5) Marshalls; **78-79** All Sarah Cuttle; **80-81** All David Murphy, (far right) Sarah Cuttle; **82-83** (1) Mark Winwood, (2) Marshalls, (3) Westminster Stone, (4-6) Mark Winwood, (7) Mike Newton; **84** All Mark Winwood; **85** David Murphy; **86-92** All Mark Winwood; **93** (1-2) David Murphy, (3-4) Mark Winwood; **94** All Mark Winwood; **95** David Murphy; **96-97** All Sarah Cuttle (bottom right) Mark Winwood; **98-103** All Sarah Cuttle; **104-109** All Mark Winwood; **110** (1-6) Mark Winwood, (bottom right) Sarah Cuttle; **111** All Sarah Cuttle; **112-113** (far left) Mike Newton, (1-8) Mark Winwood; **114-115** All Luxform; **116** All Mark Winwood; **117** All David Murphy; **118-119** All Mark Winwood; **120** All Sarah Cuttle; **121** All Mark Winwood

acknowledgements

TOMMY'S

An enormous thanks to my wife Marie for having to type up every word of my often illegible scribble onto the PC. Georgie Bennett, Richard Foy, Micky Cunningham and Jimmy the Joiner for vital information! To Ruth, Angela, Brad, Amanda, David, Sarah, Anthony, Neal, Sarah C. and Andres for their help and patience in co-ordinating and stitching together this book! And a special thanks to my old friends Guy and Sarah at B&Q for all their help supplying goods for this book. Also a big thank you to Julie Ryan and Dennis Burnham at Capel Manor* for letting us use their gardens and a chance to meet all the future landscapers! Thank you to Linda Robichaud for letting me play with the WoodBlocX. And to Amanda Patton** for for the use of her garden designs.

FOR AIREDALE PUBLISHING

We would like to thank the following companies for providing tools and equipment for this book:

FOR EVERYTHING FROM A–Z

Guy Burtenshaw, Sarah Stonebanks at B&Q and all the very patient staff at B&Q Yeading

FOR TOOLS AND EQUIPMENT

Trevor Culpin at Screwfix Direct for tools
Suzanne Mills at Atlas Copco for tools
Nick Cook at DeWalt for tools
Stuart Elsom at Rollins Group for tools
Wacker GB Limited for loan of a Wacker Compactor
Deidre and John Kelly at Source box for Luxform Lighting
Julie Doyle at Crown Paint
Ian Lincoln at Jewsons, Leytonstone
Linda Robichaud at WoodBlocX
Lorraine Willis at Rolawn for turf
Also thanks to the following for their help in the production of this book: *Claire Graham and Tom Newton for use of their gardens. Antony Cairns and Alexa Seligman for that extra help*

*CAPEL MANOR horticultural college, gardens open to the public **tel:** 0208 366 4442 **email:** enquiries@capel.ac.uk **web:** www.capel.ac.uk ****AMANDA PATTON GARDEN DESIGN tel:** 01963210882 **web:** www.amandapatton.co.uk